MW00940095

Still Outside the Wire

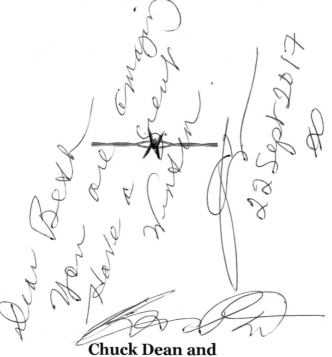

Chuck Dean and
Bridget C. Cantrell, PhD.

Still Outside the Wire

Still Outside the Wire
Copyright © 2017
Charles A. Dean, Bridget C. Cantrell

All rights reserved. No part of this book may be reproduced, stored in a retrieval system, or transmitted in any form or by any means—electronic, mechanical, photocopying, recording, or otherwise—without prior permission in writing from the copyright holder except as provided by USA copyright law.

Printed in the United States of America

What We May Never Know

"In time, we will know how many billions of dollars have been spent on the wars. We will know how many soldiers have been wounded, how many arms and legs lost, how many skulls shattered and how many spines severed. We will know how many men and women have returned in coffins draped with the flag.

We may even learn how many of our people come home to a marriage they can no longer maintain, a job they can no longer hold, a society they no longer feel comfortable in, a life they can no longer bear to live. In time, we may even know which divorces, which lives sinking into alcohol and drugs and which suicides had roots in Fallujah or Baghdad or Kabul.

What we can never know—and I speak for all Americans who have never been to war—is the experience, or accumulation of experiences, that damages soldiers invisibly, yet so deeply that we label their pain with an acronym they must share with rape victims, automobile accident victims,

Still Outside the Wire

victims of robbery or abuse. PTSD: post-traumatic stress disorder.

We can only guess at what specifically induced it in those men and women, sons and daughters. Did he watch a brother-in-arms die? Was it the RPG, or the IED, that turned his HumVee to shards and his squad to KIAs? Was it the carnage? The thump of rockets? The unrelenting fear? Or did he kill? Is that what haunts him?

If past wars are any guide, it may be years—decades—before our younger veterans understand why they aren't the same people they were when they shipped out. But, if past wars are a guide, we can measure with relative certainty what many of them will go through on that path to understanding. And as bleak as that measurement may seem at times, is it not our duty to the men and women who make it their duty to fight our country's battles that we not only let them know what they may be in for, but that we provide them every allowance of help they need?...While the enemy, the terrain or the tactics may change, the aftermath doesn't."

Excerpted from the Boise Weekly November 8, 2008 by Bill Cope

**DEDICATED TO THE
EVERLASTING WARRIOR**

Still Outside the Wire

1.

The Wire

"When I packed my bags and walked out to join the Marines I never expected to find myself on the outside looking in when I got home. My family and I happily re-connected and we all felt the love but, and I hate to say this, I was really looking for something else; I wanted them to understand me in a different way. I wanted them to know what I went through. It sounds weird but I wanted them to feel the suffering me and my buddies did over there, but knowing that will never happen gives me a real lonely feeling now. With all that it's hard to feel like I'm really home...sort of like I'm still outside the wire."

You're a warrior, and when you returned to civilian life it seems like just one high hurdle after another. You were not prepared for the impact of coming home and finding that your experiences have unexpectedly changed so many areas of your life. You quickly find that the extraordinary life-changing situations, like constant life-threatening events, are impossible for anyone who has never been there to really "get it". As much as you dreamed about making it home (*and back to square one*) everything has changed. For you, everything has become different while those who stayed home go about their lives as they always had. In the wake of all these life-altering episodes you have become a part of a solitary crowd of men and women in our military that acquire a special kind of loneliness; one that is unexpected—and hard to understand. It is this aftershock that inadvertently thrusts a warrior, to one degree or another, to the other side of the wire—and creates obstacles in the path of returning one hundred percent back to the life he or she had before.

As far as loneliness goes; warriors don't mind being alone with their experiences—they usually accept that as part of the package. However, what most of them secretly long for is to have others understand the profound ways in which their experiences have impacted every moment of their waking lives. That's a tall order because even though they crave true empathy from others, they also know it is impossible to get any meaningfully input from anyone who was not there. Despite the best efforts and intentions of friends and loved ones, warriors can easily be made to feel like aliens in their own communities—strangers in a familiar land.

"Outside the wire" is military jargon for being beyond the relatively safe confines of a base camp or support installation, which makes it the perfect portrayal for us to use in this book. *Outside the wire,* simply put, is the distance a returning warrior may feel between him and the world he once knew. Experienced combat soldiers know what outside the wire means, and it seems that when people become warriors, and leave the sanctity of a peaceful civilian life, they step outside the wire—and coming back in is a tough thing to do.

So what are we talking about here? In this writing how are we using this jargon? We have found that there is no better way to explain, or describe, one of the most prevalent transitional issues amongst our returning troops; which is—the feeling of being disconnected from normal life after it is all over.

Does it affect every warrior? In some ways, yes...but many make the transition well enough after the war that most residual effects are barely noticeable. Yet others get so hung up on the outside they seem to be forever affected by their war experiences—but most are somewhere in between.

Many war-hardened troops travel through the motions of "ordinary" life, and do so with a marked sense of unreality, and maybe with only a few slight manifestations. However, the little quirks they came home with can still be representative of *being outside the wire*. Of course some warriors find themselves so far on the outside that they become experientially detached and removed from everyone and everything around them. These powerful traits are what we mean by being "outside the wire". They have been found to pose enormous obstacles in the path of reintegrating back into civilian life for many of our veterans.

Please note that being outside the wire does not always mean that a veteran is living in the wilds as a hermit, or what is better known as a "tripwire vet". There are comparatively few that have gone to that extreme, but the fact remains that most veterans will always have shades of being outside the wire as a result of surviving the horrors of war. By understanding what that really means is an objective of this book.

As for the makeup of this idea of being *outside the wire* it can be as simple as getting overly uptight over matters that are seemingly small to most civilians. Maybe it's just getting tense because someone misplaced something that is important to you, and the tension causes you to go into a "funk" that shuts you down emotionally; maybe for an inordinate amount of time. Or, perhaps it is something like the *avoidance* of driving down a particular street on garbage day because the black plastic bags remind you of body bags.

On a personal note, one of my (Chuck) particular quirks was getting compliments. I finally became aware of this some fifteen years after coming home from Vietnam. For some reason I had the toughest time receiving a compliment and would do anything to avoid them...even to the point of getting angry or rude in social settings. The reaction was a smoke screen to get everyone's attention off of me. I made sure to do what I could to downplay and mask it all over. I was, to that degree, living outside the wire.

As we go along in this book one of our main goals is to explain exactly what elements make up the construction of this "wire". Our topic is war stress of course, but within that there are many details that need to be discussed in order to get where we want to go, and the first and foremost item to discuss is PTSD.

Post-Traumatic Stress Disorder, along with traumatic brain injury, shattered nerves, debilitating guilt and the many other troubling wartime conditions have one thing in common...they can happen to anyone in any war, and any era. Those troops that ran up the beaches in Normandy in the face of massive enemy fire and bombardment, to the jungle hilltops in Vietnam, to running a convoy down a road with IEDs planted everywhere in Iraq, Syria, and Afghanistan all may find themselves reacting to life around them with startle effect, and unusual behavior. They are responding normally. They are reacting according to what they have experienced. Their survival instincts have been honed by the conditions of war—and war itself is a very abnormal human experience for any human being.

One particular way that I have found to receive some comfort, and a bit of healing, was when I realized that I was not the only one with some of these "quirks". As I began listening to other veterans' stories and accounts, there was a kind of catharsis that occurred in my heart when realizing I was not alone with what I held inside. In light of that, let's take a look at what some others have experienced. Here is one Vietnam veteran's narrative. It is easy for most of us to relate:

"Soon after getting back from 'Nam, I found myself sleeping with a K-bar under my pillow. I had loaded weapons around my bedroom and all over the house. I felt it absolutely necessary. I went through situations where I ended up pulling these weapons on people because I was startled in the night.

I watch all the time where others are. People scare me because they don't know that the things they do trip my wire. I'm afraid I'll react and dust them off without being able to stop myself. Know what I mean?

'Nam is like a disease—it just keeps eating away at my insides. I'd like to talk to someone about these things, but I don't think there's anyone interested in talking about hell.

Life is rose-colored glasses if you've been to 'Nam. I once tried talking to a friend about it, but all he gave me was an "understanding" smile and a blank look. I'll never do that again because it made me end up hating him...and I've had enough hate for a lifetime."

This is a typical, though somewhat extreme, account for many vets. Here is another one that illustrates the (not so extreme) subtlety of being outside the wire:

"The first couple of months on the ground were not so bad. However, things gradually got worse. It started with RPG attacks, then rocket attacks and finally I.E.D.s; they are the scariest and nastiest things I have ever seen. They explode out of nowhere and are filled with nails, screws, bolts and whatever else that will tear through body armor and flesh.

I gradually became more and more fearful. Every day was spent wondering if today was going to be my day, and if so, would it be painful or would it be quick? When a couple of friends were hit with I.E.D. blasts outside our living quarters, I suddenly realized that I did not want to be in a war any longer. As I looked down at the casualties I was too terrified to move or help, and I stood frozen as I watched people running around screaming, "medic". When I finally went into action I discovered that most of the guys had minor shrapnel wounds. One of them, however, had taken the brunt of the blast and I had to watch him choke to death on his own blood. There was nothing I could do except sit and watch as someone I had trained with for two years slowly die. To add more misery to this, our squad had switched patrols that night with the one who was hit. If we had gone on the normally scheduled patrol I would have been sitting in the same seat, and I would have been the casualty instead of my friend. All I wanted to do was go home. I wanted it all to end, but even now that I am home there still is no end. Not a day goes by that I do not have images of that awful scene."

Those images in this warrior's mind will always be there. Perhaps we can lay out some tools for you if you have some similar feelings. Understanding more about what's going on will help make a transit across the wire easier as time goes on.

Still Outside the Wire

2.

There Will be Wars

"War is hell. We can only stuff our past experiences inside for so long before they begin to eat their way to the surface. The war never ends but it seems like no one can see that but us. To me that's the biggest letdown of all, and it feels like I'm living outside the wire looking at life as it goes by on the other side. I don't really know how to get over there. Coming home is as much hell as going to war."
—A Veteran of G.W.O.T.

In 2009, "Nat" of the 101st Airborne Division returned stateside from his first combat deployment. In Afghanistan he had seen firsthand the carnage of explosions set off in crowded street markets. Back on base at Fort Campbell, Kentucky, he tried to put those memories behind him. But echoes of wartime still haunted him as he as he inched through the commissary one day soon after returning home.

He made his way through the market with his back to the aisles' shelves, keeping a watchful eye on the bustle. Children toddled behind their mothers, sometimes squealing or crying. Nat couldn't stand the crying.

Then a thought hit him, coursing through his body it hit him like an electric current: *All of these people are going to die!* His eyes darted around the fluorescent-lit store as the dread grew. I'm going to see them all die, he thought...any minute now.

Nat had taken his back off the shelves just long enough to turn a corner when a man bumped into him from behind. Before Nat knew what happened, the man was in the air. The next moment he was on the ground, sprawled on his back, looking up at Nat incredulously. What had transpired was still crystallizing in Nat's mind as he sheepishly apologized, offered his hand to help the man up, and excused himself from the store. He had just experienced a PTSD-related flashback. To this day, he doesn't have a clear memory of what happened in the commissary. The unexpected bump from a stranger triggered combat memories, and he says his mind was transported back to the crowded Afghan markets where he had witnessed explosion after explosion.

Sitting in his parked car outside the store Nat watched the military police pull up. Then he drove off. That's when he decided to stop going out. For the sake of others, he told himself, he'd stay home. There, he found temporary relief from his unrelenting hyper vigilance: alcohol and a heavy-duty regimen of military-prescribed painkillers, anti-anxiety drugs, and sleep medications. The cocktail of pills and liquor rendered him incapacitated most of the time. Nat was on the other side of the wire all the time with no answers on how to come back in.

***

War is something shared by many. The reactions to it are common amongst the troops who serve in it, and there is a certain degree of peace each troop gets by just knowing that he or she isn't alone. The objective of this book is help you come home and get on with your life in a productive way. Sadly, however, many warriors believe that by admitting to unwanted feelings or personal problems stemming from their wartime experiences that they are showing signs of weakness. This is not true, and in fact is just the opposite. The soldier who has a problem, but can't admit it, lives in fear—fear that someone may consider him less than he is.

One thing for certain war affects our lives like no other phenomena. It generates a sense of anxiety that can destroy our peace of mind, and it can create fears that wake us in the night and intrude on our thoughts during the day. It can break our ability to concentrate while we work and while we play. War's effects can turn small problems into huge issues. For the survivors, the ravages of war have a profound impact on their lives, and it robs them of their personal sense of control and security. In short, war creates a tremendous amount of stress. If it goes unrecognized and unmanaged, this stress can severely damage mental and physical health.

Throughout history the general costs tallied from war are things like lost territory, number of cities destroyed, and governments toppled. Little interest has been shown regarding the after-shock soldiers go through. Rarely are their stressful reactions understood. Millions of individual combatants around the world (not just the U.S.) "live outside the wire", and continue to be in need of support concerning their wartime experiences. Theirs is the neglected "human factor" of war. Unfortunately, this always seems to be the last casualty remembered when counting the costs of wars.

War stress lives in a soldier's history of war. It's a history that until recently has been hidden from view, and poorly documented. The individual soldier's system of reporting the historical facts, and how he felt after the impacting circumstances of combat, has not been easy to record. War experiences are generally held in quiet confidentiality by most soldiers and have been a puzzling secret kept from those who were not there to also experience it. These experiences have presented a perplexing question for war historians over the years, as well as a gap of alienation that occurs between the warrior and the rest of the world.

Within the great and special "secret" of war exists the darkest corner of all...war's essential feature: *Combat*. Only the individual soldier who has lived through it can really report, with any accuracy, what it is like to survive the emotionally rigorous circumstances that arise from the field of combat. Likewise, it is extremely difficult for the soldiers to relate these experiences to anyone who has not been there, making therapy and remedies from the professional communities almost impossible. Unless the therapist is also ex-military, with relative experiences, he or she will find the veteran unwilling to be completely open for many suggested remedies and/or treatment.

From the present war on terror we are seeing some peculiar, and yet familiar, after affects coming home with the troops. "Familiar" because it is not so unlike many of the warning signs which manifested as the troops came home from Vietnam back in the 60's and 70's. Following is a couple of sad news excerpts that poignantly frame the problems:

"The three special operations soldiers (at Ft. Bragg) who investigators say killed their wives had been deployed to Afghanistan for the war on terrorism..."

Fayetteville Observer — July 2002

"In a tragic footnote to war, some Marines returning from combat in Iraq are losing their lives to risky behavior such as speeding and driving drunk. Throughout the Marine Corps, 31 service members have died in nonmilitary vehicle accidents since late April, when troops began trickling back home.

The numbers spiked in June, when at least one Marine a week was killed in car and motorcycle crashes..."
San Diego Union Tribune — September 2003

What is behind this risky behavior? When people train and go to war they deploy with a high sense of survival, and the adrenaline may run non-stop for weeks on end. This goes beyond a normal human activity (typical of post-traumatic stress) and when it runs that long it is hard to turn off. Once the excitement and danger of war is over, and the troops come home, many seek out ways to continue to behave in a way that keeps the adrenaline running...if they don't, they will "come-down" from the high. Once they are down they may have to confront things that the rush has diverted them from.

Veterans can watch the physical wounds heal up, but the scars on the flesh are merely reminders of former pain and suffering that came during the war. As time goes by the flesh wounds heal but the wounds in the mind are unseen, and remain an affliction that continues to cause problems.

Stress is a personal response that our bodies and minds have in order to meet the demands of the different situations in life that we are presented with. If these situations happen to go beyond the range of normal human experiences (and war trauma is certainly something beyond that range), then we become particularly vulnerable to having severe symptoms of what is known as Post-Traumatic Stress Disorder (commonly called PTSD). PTSD is a reaction to the extreme stress that we encountered during war. With PTSD readjusting to civilian life is made tougher.

Military personnel are trained and conditioned to survive constant life-threatening situations. However, this training can become a stumbling block in returning back to normal civilian life. Upon trying to readjust to "normal" life, many situations can become a matter of survival for those who have been forward deployed. Sometimes we react in a combat mode to get the job done and survive;

the civilian world finds it difficult to understand these responses.

Modern war is producing more survivors than previous wars. Because of the advancement in medicine and transportation methods for the wounded, many who may have died in earlier times are now coming home to get on with their lives. This causes one of the most predominant forms of stress—survivor's guilt. Living outside the wire comes hand in hand with this phenomenon.

In order to survive in a war soldiers undergo a radical reduction in their sense of the actuality of things. This naturally happens so the warrior may avoid losing his or her senses completely. This phenomenon is called "shut down," or numbness of feeling and emotion; and even though a warrior who has returned from war is mingling with the crowd—it does not necessarily mean that he has come in from living outside the wire. Unbeknownst to them the primary task of combat warriors returning home is to find their way to the other side of the wire—to embrace becoming a civilian once again.

The transition from civilian life to military life and then back again, is challenging to say the least. By joining the military we as civilians lose many freedoms that were once taken for granted—such as choice and mobility, just to name a couple. Suddenly new warriors must submit to forceful commanding authorities—perhaps for the first time in their life. And in order to adapt to the military mindsets, and lifestyle, they must rapidly discover and develop what it takes to adjust properly to their challenging new environment. Here's a short son-to-father communiqué that has far-reaching implications:

"Dear Dad,
I've personally blown up five Iraqi tanks in the air sorties that I've flown over here. I know there were people inside those tanks, Dad, but I can't afford to think about that right now and still do my job. I know for certain that when I get home

Still Outside the Wire

I'll have to face who was inside those tanks. I'm not looking forward to that." A U.S. Pilot, Kuwait liberation 1991

During a wartime situation a new and even more intense transition is added to a warrior's life—the transition from conditions of peace and security to the conditions of danger and vulnerability. This transition brings about further conflicts, which add to the emotional burden of the individual. The danger of being wounded, or even killed, is clear and tangible. This becomes a constant drain on their emotional state, and the pressure and fear can bring out many impulses that create lasting impressions...some good, and others not so good. These times of stress can be the cause of many negative issues, and the longer they remain unprocessed the longer a warrior remains outside the wire.

While serving, and as time moves on, warriors develop an intense feeling of pride, honor, and solidarity with the people in their unit. The feeling of responsibility for the fate of others contributes much to the motivation to press on in the fight. Consequently, one of the most painful aspects of coming home from war and reintegrating back to civilian life is leaving that unit camaraderie that has been carved out with blood, sweat, and tears.

Each member in the unit changes within themselves according to the demands placed upon them, both as individuals and participants, of a team. It is then that we learn how to live through extraordinary hardships together, and we cared that everyone made it through. We passed around the same rain-soaked cigarettes from man to man and no one was left out. Together we sweltered in desert heat and learned to like MREs or out-of-date C-rations. We were satisfied with snuggling up and sleeping in the driest part of a wet fighting hole—and perhaps even trying to stay warm in the arms of someone who had been a perfect stranger only days before. In the most primal conditions we, as warriors, come to know each other's inner characters. We do this through many-shared hardships. In the midst of it all we see one another's human weaknesses and amazing strengths as we work as a team to overcome the rigors and horrors of war.

No matter how bad the conditions were, or how often we dreamed of returning home to a normal life, to leave our close-knit intimate group (our buddies) was a difficult task indeed. What we had seen and done with our comrades for those many long months could never be replaced in one's heart. When we left, it was like a tearing in our souls. This feeling of "community" is what veterans long for when they get home—they want to belong once again to something beyond them; they want to bond and trust in civilian life the same as they did in the war zone. We believe if that can be re-established in civilian life then many of the prevailing re-adjustment issues may begin to dissipate.

***

Perhaps one of the most important tools in dealing with the wire and getting back across in good order is to understand what reaching "middle ground" means.

During our time on active duty most of us never received any instruction on how to negotiate a peaceful resolution with anyone especially those we considered to be "the" enemy. In war, we had only one job—that was to close with the enemy and eliminate him. When we could not neutralize or overcome the opposing force we could retreat. If the enemy could be eliminated then we would continue the attack. From the earliest time that man began to strategize, and make war, this has been the military way.

We were trained in this manner...it was all we knew. Fight or flight—live or die—win or lose. When we return to civilian life many of us do not let go of our old ways of thinking—keeping us outside the wire. When situations get intense, some of us resort to what we know best...fight like hell or run the other direction, and escaping to the outer reaches of the wire and staying there. We know little about reaching middle ground in the midst of conflict.

It is easy to see that this behavior is not conducive to making good lasting relationships in a civilian world. With relationships we must not avoid conflicts, but rather seek to resolve them. In the process, if things go well, our relationships will be strengthened and not crippled. We will come away with a stronger understanding of ourselves and the ones we love. When we successfully resolve conflicts we come away feeling like a team that has tackled and overcome an adversary as one unit; and we are stronger as a result. Either we can ignore our worsening condition with those around us, or we can forge new paths in reaching "middle ground" where peaceful resolutions can occur. As we do, we will go far in making a safe and healthy transition back across the wire.

As wartime veterans, though our patterns may be firmly entrenched, it is never too late to make adjustments for changes. We can choose to learn new skills in coping and resolving conflicts peacefully, and when we do the days ahead will be more productive and pleasant for everyone involved—the choice is ours.

Many combat veterans must work hard to allow other people to get close—even their own families. Enduring wartime experiences can cause us to subconsciously surround ourselves with a firewall (the wire). We think that this self-protective mechanism will help us prevent any more emotional suffering and pain. It is our inner person saying, "I've had enough!"

We refer to this mechanism as stringing up the "perimeter wire". It is an invisible barrier of concertina wire used to keep others away. It maintains a comfortable distance. Not because the warrior does not love those around him or her, but because they are afraid to bring them into their combat-riddled heart. There is a fear that if you allow them all the way into your heart, and if something happens to them (like what happened to close comrades in war), then the hurt would be too intense to endure and you may not be able to take it.

The following is another view of how the wire can look...especially with loved ones: *"Before I deployed down range I was different about my wife and kids. Now that I'm back I can only let them get so close before I have to get away from them. I used to have fun letting my boys jump and crawl all over me. We would spend hours playing like that. Now I can only take a couple of minutes of it before I have to get out. I usually get in my truck and drive back to the base to be with my platoon."*

That statement by a U.S. GWOT warrior just back from northern Iraq is a classic example of this wire being in place and not understanding it. The young sergeant shared this dilemma with us while we helped some troops in Italy re-integrate after their tour of duty. He came to us seeking answers and wanted to know why he had so little tolerance now for being around his small children. Their high energy had not bothered him before going off to war, but now it was too much for him. He was confused and distraught because he loves his kids and did not understand why he now had such a mysterious "distance" toward them.

We knew what he was going through. The moment that he told us he had to get away, and usually felt best (safe) when he was at the base with his buddies, we saw the reflection of many veterans like him. When we described our understanding of what he was experiencing, and shared something similar examples of what I (Chuck) had gone through after coming home from Vietnam, we could see the relief he needed. I told him about the wire I had strung up around me after coming home.

So how does this wire get strung into place? How do we string it up so that it creates such a blocking effect on relationships?

We do it by subconscious decisions. When explained to the sergeant that in the heat of battle, or a life-threatening experience, it is common to make vows...and perhaps even bargain a little with God, the lights came on for him. We talked about the times when we witness people (who are close to us) getting hurt or killed, and how easy it is to decide that it may not be worth the emotional pain to allow people to get close to us ever again. We explained that usually to avoid future pain the computation says that it is best not to get close to anyone—and that is the "wire" we string up. It is there to keep us from feeling any more emotional pain caused by the war. We have created a "no-man's land" between us and the rest of the world—and it is there primarily to protect others who are trying to get too close.

***

In respect to the closeness that is natural to families we must always consider what all of this is doing to family members as well. As a child of a veteran, I (Bridget) saw first-hand what it is like to grow up in a home with a father who was tormented by traumatic memories. His combat experiences came home with him after World War II and the Korean Conflict, and they became a part of our family for many years. In so many ways I now can recognize how much he lived outside the wire.

I also know what it is like to be a product of an environment where the amplification of emotions run rampant. The intensity of these emotions is more often than not intimidating, unpredictable, and frightening for the loved ones.

Family members living with veterans are many times left feeling helpless and reluctant to communicate. Stress reactions such as these are certainly not conducive to building intimacy and close-knit family units.

Not only do I have a personal experience of growing up with a father who had Post Traumatic Stress Disorder (PTSD), but also a father who was determined to gain insight into his behavior and develop more adaptive ways of dealing with his anger and stress reactions. He was my role model in confirming that it is never too late to make amends and change the old patterns of one's journey.

Having been fortunate enough to see the world from these eyes, I now devote my work to veterans and their family members. It is immensely rewarding helping them understand the dynamics and effects of trauma reactions. I take great pleasure seeing loved ones working together as a team to overcome the debilitating effects that are sometimes associated with trauma. It is my hope that this book will offer some fresh new perspectives in developing more effective tools for coping with the aftermath of trauma. Hopefully it will also be a travel-friendly roadmap for your passage to the other side of the wire and back home.

3.

Global War on Terror—
the Everlasting Hell

"It all ended with my leg being amputated. I did my service in Afghanistan in 1979. Wounded in July, I was admitted to the hospital at the same time. I did not realize at the hospital that I was a disabled man, because everyone there is crippled in some fashion or another. It wasn't until I returned home to Moscow that it occurred to me that my life was never going to be the same again.

I met my old friends; they were all healthy and their lives were full of interesting things. I realized then that a lot would be missing from my own life, and I must confess that I gave up. I started drinking a lot and used drugs whenever I had the chance to get them.

In the hospital in Afghanistan the anesthetics they gave me were narcotic, and soon the doctors realized that I could not do without them. They helped me go through addiction withdrawal. But once back in Moscow I found myself under a lot of stress and began to use them again. It was the only way that I could keep from thinking about the war, my dead friends, and the loneliness of being a used up soldier with no civilian skills.

If I had not gone to war none of this would have happened. It has scarred me in other places besides my body. My wife would not have divorced me and I would not have lost my family. If she only knew what I went through in Afghanistan...I think she believes that I was on a holiday, basking in the sun and taking hikes in the countryside. I just can't seem to relate to others anymore, and I am sure they don't understand me either. If only I had not gone to war..." A Russian "Afghantsi" Veteran.

This kind of darkness I had seen before. It reminded me of coal dust lifting off a miner's back as he emerges from a day's work deep in the bowels of the earth. However, Sergei's dusky aura was not so easily shaken off and he seemed to be sheathed by it. As he walked toward me in the hotel lobby I could not see the invisible black veil that was preventing him from feeling the world around him, but I knew it was there. He brought it home from the war in Afghanistan. Some vet buddies of his told me he lives outside the wire—and didn't have a battle plan on how to come back in. I had heard that many times before and know it's the result of the murky cloud that surrounded him—but what to do about it?

He and I (Chuck) had agreed to meet through the arrangement of his friends in the Afghanistan Veterans Union, in Minsk, Belarus. The year was 1992, and I was impressed at how much these veterans cared about one another. Their war was not much different than mine in Vietnam. It was a long drawn out guerilla-type affair, unpopular at home, and we had very few meaningful reasons for being there. Then we returned home in defeat.

Sergei saw a good deal of combat during his time in Afghanistan. Some incidents in particular had never left his mind—like the horrifying sight of Viktor, a close comrade and friend, being blown-up by a land-mine. Even when he returned to Belarus these images haunted him. Scenes from battle would run repeatedly through his mind and disrupt his focus so much that he couldn't do his work and was laid off. Even filling up at the gas station the smell of diesel would immediately rekindled certain horrific memories. At other times, he had difficulty remembering the past—as if some events were too painful to be allowed back into his mind. His girlfriend complained that he was always pent-up and irritable—as if he were on guard, and Sergei noticed that at night he had difficulty relaxing and falling asleep. When he heard loud noises, such as a truck back-firing, he would literally jump and ready himself for combat. He began to drink heavily and found himself avoiding socializing with old military buddies because it would inevitably trigger a new round of memories. Thankfully his fellow veterans at the Union embraced him, and in response he began the long journey home. That's when we met.

Later I learned that Sergei had come to our meeting with expectations. He had hopes that I could show him a pathway out of the long dark night of the soul. To this day I hope I helped even a little with his quest. When I left Russia a few weeks later I did notice the overcast veneer surrounding him was beginning to fade, and that he had perked up with even the occasional smile. With PTSD one can only hope for the best, but I did take it all with a certain degree of accomplishment. Not being a clinician, with professional tools, I simply did what I found to be successful in helping 'Nam Vets over the years: I tried to help him gain some understanding of the unconscious mechanisms that war can put into place. I do feel that by shining enough light on what was going on with his thoughts and responses to life, that it did help him finally pierce the cloak.

It seems that the Steppes are the hardest places to fight a war. Afghanistan is a testimony to that, and our military forces are now finding that out every day of the year. Whether or not Russia's war in Afghanistan can be considered part or partial of the Global War on Terror may be stretching it some, but in any case there are so many similarities in then and now that it cannot be totally pushed to the side—especially with the lessons and effects that it has had on the warriors who fight there. There are many important parallels, and one thing for certain PTSD has no nationality, creed, or ideology. It can happen to anyone who experiences the tremendous horrors of war.

"Somebody was waiting at home for each of us. Parents, friends, wives, children. But why did the best among us so often turn out to be the ones who were killed, while the bastards kept coming back? They returned

home in order to pound on their chest and yell that I, the shit, spilled blood in Afghanistan. Only the blood was not his own, but somebody else's...the blood of those who came here for nothing and were killed for no one. The blood of those who came here as children and returned as old men. Who will answer for this blood?" Those familiar words and thoughts were written in a powerful and moving book by Vladislav Tamarov, a Soviet Afgan veteran, titled "Aghanistan: A Russian Soldier's Story".

I (Chuck) met Vlad Tamarov in 1992 soon after my trip to Russia. He was sent my way by the Afghanistan Veterans Union of Minsk, Belarus. Vlad is an extremely talented person in many fields of the arts. Even though he was a mine sweeper in the special services he did not let the war interfere with his creativity as a photographer. He returned to homeland Russia with some stunning photographs taken during his long strenuous time in Afghanistan. He also came home with PTSD.

Vlad came to my home for a visit soon after I returned from Russia. We got to know one another fairly well and found many things in common; one being the fact that we shared likenesses in the aftereffects of a war. His war, like mine in Vietnam, was one that made no sense, was not won, and very unpopular at home. Thinking back now we both were certainly camped outside the wire and searching for a way to cross over. We both have since done much better and made headway, but we know that what was imbedded in our psyche from the experience will always be there. War is war, no matter what uniform one wears.

So here we are in present time and ironically America finds itself trapped in the revolving door of an Afghanistan war—and the Russians have left. Back then we sided with the Mujahedeen, who have the same ideals, etc. as the Taliban, and helped them win their war. Due to our support they defeated Russia and its Afghanistan proxy government, and then as the world turned, and 9/11 occurred, we returned to engage nearly identical forces that we had helped in their own fight just a few short years before. A vicious cycle; this is the ugly face of the global war on terror.

Russia's departure left it wide open for the Taliban to conquer and rule from 1996 to 2001 when U.S. forces came back and ousted them. 28 April 1992 marks the date the Mujahedeen celebrated their victory over the Red Army forces in Afghanistan. The original Mujahedeen of the 1980s and today's Taliban may use the same language of holy war, but their understanding of jihad is worlds apart. The key difference between the original Mujahedeen and the Taliban is that the former waged a traditional type of jihad. In a traditional jihad, if waged locally, a contest over control of resources takes place between rival strongmen who each run their own private armies. In this scenario, the ultimate legitimacy to rule draws upon military strength, but the contest itself is called jihad simply because Islam is the sole language of political legitimacy.

At any rate, a war in Afghanistan seems to be everlasting and unwinnable. The Afghanistan area has been invaded many times in recorded history, but no invader has been able to control all of its regions at the same time, and at some point faced rebellion. Some of the invaders in the history of Afghanistan include Genghis Khan, Alexander the Great, and various Persian Empires. Then came the British, the Soviet Union, and most recently, a coalition force of NATO troops—the majority from the United States.

As a result, our weary troops are now experiencing the anguish of a seemingly unending revolving door of redeployments. More than ever we need to support them in ways that will make lasting differences in their transitions. This book, "Outside the Wire" is one of those ways to help the troops and their loved ones make positive and sustainable transitions from war to peace.

4.

War is Declared

To Iraq and Back—GWOT (Global War on Terror). President George W. Bush first used the term "War on Terror" on 20 September 2001...and GWOT officially began. The terrorist attacks of 9/11 drew America fully into this shadowy war that seems to have no end. For reasons still to be determined, the President made a decision to launch the war in Iraq instead of a full scale effort in Afghanistan to bring Osama bin Laden to justice. This radical madman had publicly taken credit for the attacks on the U.S. but we went elsewhere with a huge military campaign. Whether or not any political decision is right or wrong, our interest lies (in this book) with the fact that thousands of American troops have been subjected to the horrors of war, and all the ramifications that result from that experience.

Ask any veteran how life is after war. Most likely in their own words (and ways) they will tell you how it imprinted lasting marks on their minds and souls. Some may let you know all the different ways their war never ends. On the other hand, many will not even begin to talk about it because they feel nobody would ever understand unless they had been there too. For people back home, who have never experienced war, it is vital that they understand that it is difficult to fathom how things have changed for the returning troops.

In some ways the war in Iraq was much like the war in Vietnam. One of the primary similarities is that there were no front lines, and you could be attacked at any time—anywhere. "Mortaritaville" was a classic example of that in the war in Iraq. Let us give you a brief flavor of what it was like:

The Department of Defense designated it as Logistical Support Area (LSA) Anaconda, but the troops called it "Mortaritaville". They called it that because it averaged more than 50 incoming rocket or mortar attacks monthly. Americans were routinely wounded or killed by these attacks. Camp Anaconda was near Balad Airbase, which is one of the most secure bases that the U.S. had in Iraq...and it was big. As of May 2004, Anaconda had 17,000 troops and was 12 1/2 miles in circumference. Similar to the large base camps in Vietnam.

The 4,000 troops in the 3rd Brigade Combat Team, 4th Infantry Division, had nine forward operating bases spread across 1,500 square miles of Iraq north of Baghdad, from Samarra to Taji. The unit was headquartered at Logistics Support Area Anaconda.

(The following is a first-hand account by an individual soldier at LSA Anaconda.)

"On the night of July 3rd, 2003, American forces were attacked in two separate incidents at Balad Airbase. The well-coordinated ambushes injured 18 American

soldiers and left 11 Iraqi fighters dead. The attacks involved typical guerilla weapons such as machine guns and rocket-propelled grenades, as well as a new element—highly accurate mortars that can be fired from as far away as 6.5km. In one attack on a highway near Balad, U.S. soldiers were ambushed three times over a span of eight hours. The guerillas were armed with AK-47 assault rifles, rocket-propelled grenades and heavy machine guns.

Less than two hours before the first ambush, four mortar rounds were fired into the grounds of Camp Anaconda. A total of 16 U.S. soldiers were wounded in that attack. Two of them, members of the 4th Infantry Division, were evacuated from the area and stabilized. The rest were treated on the spot and released. This was the first instance of a mortar attack against U.S. troops since President Bush declared an end to major combat on May 1, 2003."

And the beat goes on as a harsh reality lived out by thousands of young Americans who served in the Iraqi war zone.

"Mortaritaville" was not just a big base; it was a perception. Much like the bunkers, hootches, and muddy monsoon downpours that became perceptions and icons for us in Vietnam, "Mortaritaville" became a lifelong memory for the troops who served and survived there together. America's involvement in the Iraqi war was not merely a matter of political rightness or wrongness; it was also a matter of the price we must once again pay in human lives. For the thousands of young people who fought there, Iraq will live on vividly for them forever.

While trying to stay alive at places like "Mortaritaville" troops thought and dreamed of "home" and it became a revered memory. Thinking of home, and anticipating a safe place to return created a type of solace that is critical in the mental well-being for those so far away. Several months into a combat tour, home becomes an icon of hope and almost a mythical concept that loses more of its reality the longer one is immersed in the horrors of war. In order to imagine what life will be like when returning one usually resorts to idealizing what awaits them on the home front.

Then the countdown begins. It becomes a process of counting days, hours, minutes, and seconds until one throws down the tools of war and climbs on a "freedom bird" to return home, where it is safe, clean, and comforting. Knowing, or thinking, that the war will end and they will return to peace and comfort, doesn't always happen that way.

Those who have been "down range" struggled hard to survive just to come back to the world they knew and loved. Instead many find themselves still living outside the wire. Most returning warriors expect to start all over again but going back to square one can easily escapes them. The first thing returning warriors must realize is that reintegration back home will never begin at square one again. Square one no longer exists for those who have gone to war, and coming home fully charged with stress can make it more of a letdown. This becomes apparent when a loved one asks, "What was it like?", and you look into eyes that have not seen what yours have and suddenly realize that home is farther away than you ever imagined. You come to the stark realization that you are outside the wire looking in.

In recent years I (Chuck) have volunteered at the local USO in Las Vegas. I do this for two primary reasons: First of all to support the current troops with their needs while in transit, and then to keep my hand on the pulse of their affairs as much as I can. During this time I have run into troops from all branches of the service; from several different countries. Recently I had the occasion to meet one young officer who had been an operator of the UAV aircraft (unmanned aerial vehicles capable of being remotely controlled for autonomous flight operations) at Creech AFB just north of Las Vegas. In our conversation he told me that he had transferred out of that duty because he was too stressed to continue. We do not usually consider someone who fights a war from such a distance to have stressful emotional challenges, but perhaps we aren't considering with the depth needed to be aware of the existence in these troops. He told me that day after day his duty was to stay locked onto (aerial surveillance) certain suspected individuals half-way around the world, and follow their every movement in the global fight against terrorism. He would perhaps watch this person play with his children, and do daily living routines maybe for weeks on end. He then said that he would also go home at night and play with his own kids, and go about the activities of a normal family man. Then one day his "target" became a confirmed enemy combatant and the order was given to eliminate him. He said that it was too much for him to carry on his conscious and he had to get out. He was granted a transfer to another job specialty, but what he had already experienced will live with him forever. I can only hope that he becomes aware of the *wire*—and manages to deal with it over the coming years.

As a veteran who was down range many years ago, I (Chuck) know I must find a way to make my time in Vietnam count for something more than the heartache it caused. And I (Dr.

Cantrell) as the daughter of a World War II/Korean War veteran and a therapist, who has devoted my career to working with combat trauma survivors, believe that perhaps this is the moment that both of us can offer you a guide (and the motivation) towards healing. This book is not intended to be just another book about war, but a tool to help you deal with the perimeter wire that has been put in place by it. The book is intended to help you find a way to come back to the side of the wire you were once on. Easy does it...there are some gradient steps to take in that process.

Still Outside the Wire

5.

Invisible Wounds—
An Introduction to PTSD

Many troops coming home from GWOT combat arenas like Iraq and Afghanistan suffer from the aftereffects of the experiences of surviving in a combat zone. Vehicular mobilization assignments such as convoys and urban warfare have made this war era unique. Trauma induced by these wartime activities can create vulnerability to stress reactions and result in PTSD.

Post Traumatic Stress Disorder occurs when a person has experienced, witnessed, or has been confronted with a traumatic event—an event which involved actual or threatened death or serious physical injury to themselves or others. At which point they responded with intense fear, horror, or helplessness. (APA, DSM-IV TR, 2000) The most recent primary diagnostic criteria for PTSD falls into three groups and are summarized as follows:

Re-experiencing the trauma in nightmares, flashbacks, and intrusive thoughts.

Numbing and avoidance of reminders of the trauma (avoidance of situations, thoughts and feelings, etc.).

Persistent and increased arousal (sleep difficulties, irritability, anger outbursts, startle response, etc.).

The passage of time alone usually does not heal the psychological wounds of trauma. The natural desire to withdraw from others and not talk about the experiences or difficulties associated with the traumatic event may actually make matters worse for veterans with PTSD. Painful wounds can remain exposed, open, and raw for decades without the proper help that promotes healing. These wounds go on to fester unless they are properly cared for.

Physical wounds can heal; however the emotional wounds of trauma may go unrecognized if they are never addressed. If a person attempts to slough it off by saying something like "What happened in Iraq or Afghanistan happened...that's the end of story," usually indicates that there is a deep need to receive some help in dealing with some covered-up issues—issues that may be keeping you outside the wire.

To recognize (and admit) that you may be experiencing some re-adjustment challenges is the first step to recovery. Finding useful tools to direct you and your family to constructive ways to re-adjust after war is a top priority.

PTSD Can Happen to Anyone

At one time only troops engaged in heavy direct-fire combat were even treated, observed, or evaluated for psychological problems. But since the Vietnam War, and now GWOT (where there are no real front lines), it is clearly evident that PTSD is found both in combat veterans and in many rear-echelon support troops. Likewise, it has been diagnosed in sailors who spend their entire tours off the coast on ships. It has surfaced in drone pilots and sensor operators who fight from a distance, or troops who support the war from static compounds.

These days involvement in a war takes on a completely new identity, and is not necessarily fought from the front lines, jungles, rice paddies, urban trenches, or Humvees convoying in a hot war zone. Post-Traumatic Stress Disorder can develop in service members who are engaged in GWOT... regardless of job or proximity to danger.

To recognize PTSD as a real part of war's aftereffects is vital not only for veterans, but also for the "significant others" at home. Family members, close friends, employers, etc. must obtain ample understanding about PTSD in order to help the veteran thrive in a civil society. In order for healing to begin both the veteran, and the people closest to them, need to understand and accept that this condition (PTSD) is genuine.

The very first aspect of PTSD that requires understanding is that it is not necessarily a mental illness. It is usually a normal reaction to the extreme stress encountered during your wartime experiences, and it is important to become familiar with the variety of ways it manifests after returning home.

Major Symptoms of PTSD

Listed below are some of the most primary PTSD responses veterans exhibit as a result of stress while on hardship tours and/or combat zones. (Tom Williams, Post Traumatic Stress Disorders: A Handbook for Clinicians, 1987, Appendix I). These responses are key factors in keeping a combat veteran from traversing the wire that keeps him or her alone, and on the other side:

Depression
Cynicism and distrust of government and authority
Anger
Alienation
Isolation
Sleep disturbances
Poor concentration
Tendency to react under stress with survival tactics
Psychic or emotional numbing
Negative self-image
Memory impairment
Emotional constriction
Hypersensitivity to justice
Loss of interest in work and activities
Problems with intimate relationships
Survivor guilt
Difficulty with authority figures
Hyper-alertness – hyper arousal
Avoidance of activities that arouse memories of traumas in war zone
Emotional distance from children, wife, and others

Self-deceiving and self-punishing patterns of behavior, such as an inability to talk about war experiences, fear of losing others, and a tendency to fits of rage
Suicidal feelings and thoughts
Flashbacks to dangers and combat
Fantasies of retaliation and destruction
High risk employment/recreation

Some of these post trauma responses may sound familiar. Just by acknowledging them can have healing effects for you and your loved ones. They are clues to help indicate that you may be experiencing symptoms of stress.

Still Outside the Wire

6.

Common Responses

It is important to keep it simple when looking at PTSD. Here are some helpful descriptions of the more common responses that keep a person outside the wire:

Intrusive thoughts and flashbacks. Flashbacks are a re-living of the experience as if you are there again by sight, sound, smell, or touch, and intrusive thoughts are involuntary recall of events from your traumatic past that interrupt your normal thought patterns. Daily experiences like the following scenarios can activate flashbacks or intrusive thoughts. Here are some common triggers mentioned by fellow veterans: The sound of sudden explosions, helicopters, or motorized heavy equipment. The smell of human waste and blood, diesel or jet fuel, and dirty canvas are at the top of the list. Driving on dusty sandy roads or along freeway guardrails and overpasses as well as traveling through narrow city streets can set you off. These reminders can be as subtle as hearing popcorn popping, cars backfiring, fireworks, people screaming, hot dry days, and even being caught up in large crowds of people. These examples of actual combat-related cues can be generalized into everyday living circumstances, and if you are earnest in trying to overcome the "wire" they should be studied carefully.

Isolation and avoidance. Withdrawing or isolating from social relationships emotionally or geographically, such as with family and friends can be a major problem. Avoiding activities, places, or people which reactivate traumatic memories is common. If you adopt a "leave me alone" attitude it will lead to further distance and heartache. Having the desire to become a hermit by staying outside the wire only takes you further away from the objective of re-integration. On the other hand, a healthy coping strategy is to realize that you may be able to only handle a limited amount of social interaction. It may be necessary for you to regulate your exposure in order to prevent a negative outcome (i.e. anger outbursts, excessive drinking, etc.). By using good judgment of when to avoid and when to engage may be in your best interest as well as those around you. This is the crux of being outside the wire.

Emotional numbing. This is when someone distances them self emotionally from a topic of conversation, a situation, person, or potential trigger which reminds them of a traumatic event. The traits exhibited may appear to make you seem cold, aloof, uncaring, and detached from those around you. Maybe you sometimes find yourself dissociating (checking out) in order to deal with overwhelming feelings and/or painful memories. That is actually another trip outside the wire.

The fear of losing control emotionally creates a sense of personal vulnerability. As a defense to this (and staying outside the wire) a person closes them self off in order not to feel or respond. This results in what is known as emotional numbing. You may also have difficulty controlling your reactions, which may result in anger and a desire to solve your problems with aggression. There is a prevailing fear that if one begins to feel too much of anything that they may not be able to control their emotional responsiveness. I have heard many veterans say, "If I start feeling too much, I may never stop crying, and I can't let myself go like that".

We want to encourage you to practice feeling and expressing your emotions appropriately, and when you do, over time your heart (emotions) will "thaw out" and you will feel more comfortable with where you are and what you are doing.

<u>Depression</u>. Is a common PTSD symptom as seen through the act of withdrawing and isolating from others. It can also be a result of situations in your environment that leave you feeling overwhelmed with sadness and the fear that "it" will never get better. You must hold onto the hope that over time it will get better. Sometimes it does not get better by itself and remember the "buddy system"...call a friend and have them help. (Hopefully they will be able to connect you with a trusted professional.)

There are certain behaviors associated with depression, and it is good to recognize them. When depressed one can feel helpless, hopeless, insecure, and even unworthy of being loved. Sleeping in excess is also a warning sign of depression. This need to "crash"can be seen as a way to avoid emotional pain in hopes that "it" will be gone when you wake up. Sadly avoidance of unresolved issues will never cause them to disappear, and "sleeping it off" is not the answer.

Activities which used to be fun and interesting no longer provide joy or relief from life's challenges. Your desire to make love can be greatly reduced and intimacy may not be a priority. This in itself can strain even the best of relationships. If your desire for intimacy is diminishing it may be time to get some professional guidance in this area. It can mean the survival of what is truly important to you and your partner.

At this point, you may have realized that you are depressed, and are asking, "now what?" The best place to begin is to seek out and find something to look forward to, no matter how insignificant it may seem. This is called self-care. Some good examples of self-care are: Listening to peaceful music, playing a musical instrument, reading, spending time with an animal friend, involving yourself in a hobby, getting some old fashioned exercise, or finding a trusted friend or family member you enjoy being with. And, as strange as it may seem, just getting yourself up and out of bed, taking a shower and setting yourself on a time schedule will do wonders to get you up and motivated. Begin a new chapter in your life by setting some goals.

<u>Anger</u> is basically a secondary emotion. It reflects a variety of underlying feelings such as betrayal, lack of trust, frustration, sadness, and guilt. Anger is displayed in a variety of ways (S. Akers personal communication, February 03, 2005). Anger can come on without warning, and may leave you and those around you stunned and afraid. The lack of impulse control, such as engaging in "road rage" is a real-time example of how one can get caught up in reacting to what one just experienced in a traumatic event. For example, if you were in a convoy and experienced an ambush or sudden explosion from an I.E.D., then you might find that you use road rage as a form of acting out your aggression. The reason may be, although not justified, that you have been conditioned in your combat experiences to respond in such ways that you thought helped you survive. However, this is completely unacceptable and

dangerous in a civil society. The folks back home may begin to believe that you are "crazy", and you might find yourself making excuses as to why you are not crazy. Often these road rage incidences are not even related to the event at hand; it is actually activated by the memory of a trauma you have experienced. Therefore, you revert back to the traumatic event and use the road rage as a means to vent your anger.

Anger can also be expressed non-verbally and be quite intimidating to those who are targets of your rage. I tell my vets that you have no idea how intimidating you can appear just by your body posture, and your eye contact. To appear frightening and out of control, words need not even be exchanged...therefore you must step outside yourself and look back to see just how threatening your presence and attitude can appear to others.

Domestic violence is abuse. It can manifest in many forms. Whether it be verbal, emotional, physical, or sexual; it is all abuse and not to be tolerated in any way. (Be mindful that there is NO excuse for bad behavior. PTSD does not give license for abusing others.)

Abuse stems from many sources. Low frustration tolerance with a partner or children who have no idea, or reality, as to what you have experienced while you were away, can be a leading cause in domestic violence that can land you in jail. Perhaps you have a mindset that what he or she (partner or children) does is silly and dangerous and not geared for high survival.

Likewise, domestic violence is made worse when you add alcohol and drugs to the mix. Using substances to alter your frame of mind only serves to weaken your capability to tolerate the innocent and unaware behavior of someone who has not been in a high risk situation such as combat. Remember, this is another way to end up in jail or, even worse, cause terrible injury to someone you love. If you are prone to outbursts of this nature you must take extra precaution and be committed to changing this dangerous pattern.

Anger can be used as a tactic for control and placing "your enemy" into submission. Does this sound familiar? The intensity, the volume of your voice, and the words you use are all forms of communicating your anger. Do so with good judgment.

Anger is a normal emotion, but it must be managed or it may become highly dangerous. However, with the training you have had, and the frequency at which you used anger to propel you into action, you must be aware of the downside of using it inappropriately. Remember, you are no longer in combat and these aggressive methods of expressing anger will only serve to put you at odds with your loved ones and society.

It is also unacceptable to take your anger out on objects or other living things. Breaking things, punching walls, or kicking the dog off the back porch, etc. can only lead to further alienation, shame, and embarrassment. Using aggression in the form of physical and emotional violence can take your life in the direction you do not want to go.

Take a moment to examine the patterns of how your anger is expressed. Is it expressed in the form of remaining calm before the storm? In others words, perhaps your anger percolates just below the surface as a means to mask your rage. Or maybe your anger is explosive and you may even surprise yourself with sudden outbursts.

Expressing anger by creating situations, which are contrasting to your true feelings, is called passive/aggressive anger. It is a covert anger that is hidden away while you smile and say, "no I'm not mad at you". Knowing this, it is up to you to take responsibility to manage your anger.

Some suggestions that have worked for other veterans are:

Physical exercise that is appropriate for your physical limitations
Reduce caffeine, alcohol and drug use
Relaxation/study/meditation
Well-balanced diet and rest

If you cannot do this on your own or with close relatives, it is critical that you get professional help in this area.

<u>Substance and alcohol abuse</u>. Alcohol and drugs are used regularly as a means to "self-medicate" in order to suppress feelings or memories of traumatic experiences. The reason one uses substances may be to numb the pain, forget the memories, relieve the guilt, or to just get away from it all. In reality this is a temporary fix and only serves to make things worse. Your loved ones and friends may think that you rely upon alcohol or drugs too much, and it interferes with your ability to be effective and connect with them. They are right! Your substance or alcohol use only drives you further away from your support unit (family and friends)...and you are stuck outside the wire looking in as the world goes by.

If you "use" when you first wake up and if it is the last thing you do before the end of your day, then you should seek help. The next indicator that there is a challenge in this area is when you feel you cannot make it through the day without using. It is important to do regular inventories to see if drugs and alcohol have taken over your life. Reduce your exposure to alcohol and drugs by removing it from your immediate environment. By changing your hangouts, and perhaps even those with whom you associate, may go a long way in helping you get straightened out. Every community provides some sort of recovery program to help those who struggle with inclinations to abuse substances or alcohol. We encourage you to take advantage of the resources that are available to you.

<u>Guilt.</u> You may regularly wonder why you survived when others more worthy died. You may also feel that you do not deserve to be alive, when your buddies were killed or wounded in combat and you were not. This is commonly referred to as "survivor guilt". In other words, you are blaming yourself for the outcome of something that was ultimately out

of your control. Some things need to be left in the hands of a higher power.

As a case in point I can share with you my own struggle in this area. In the late '80's I attended the opening ceremony in Sacramento that dedicated the new California Vietnam Veterans Memorial. As I approached the hundreds of names engraved on this monument I suddenly began to recognize the names of those men that I had trained as a drill instructor while serving at Ft. Ord, California in the late 60's. I began to recall the faces of my trainees, and felt responsible that perhaps they were dead because I had not failed to adequately prepare them to survive combat. I blamed myself and was overwhelmed with guilt and shame. I now realize that after many years of harboring these negative and self-destructive emotions that I did what I could to make sure they were ready for war, but accepted the fact that there were too many variables beyond my control. I had to release myself from the weight of a burden that had stuck with me for many decades. And now, when I see these brave young soldier's names inscribed on memorials I can proudly say that I had the honor of training some good men in my time.

<u>Suicidal thoughts and feelings</u>. Guilt and suicide go hand in hand. Both can cause us to act out inappropriately. Perhaps you get yourself into hopeless fights or traffic altercations as a means to punish yourself, or provoke (or fantasize) about the possibility of instigating others to do you harm (i.e. suicide by police officer, one-car accidents, etc.).

Maybe you sometimes are unable to handle "it" when things are going well, so you attempt to sabotage your success or well-being. This is an intentional setup to fail because you do not feel worthy of success. Relational suicide (intentionally blowing apart relationships with those you love or have committed to) is a very common form of self-destruction with those who have experienced war-time trauma. Take an inventory to see if you are instigating arguments that are uncalled for, which may give you reason enough to falsely justify walking away from commitments. If you are, then evaluate your priorities and re-visit the value of that relationship, as it was when you first committed. You may be surprised to find that you want to preserve what you have at all costs.

If you get to the point where you feel that life is too rough, or that maybe those you love are not able to understand you any longer, and the only way out is by taking your life, then it is time to talk! (First and foremost, it is imperative that if you feel like harming yourself or are suicidal then get professional help immediately.)

It is very important to discuss the various aspects of suicide. There are a few critical indicators that must be taken seriously. And remember, there is no "sort of suicidal"...you either are, or you are not!

Once you take the step to "check out" it is a moment of despair. I have dealt with many veterans who came to that point. They told me that before they pulled the trigger or drove their bike into an oncoming semi, they made a split second decision to live, rather than hurt those they would leave behind. Suicide is the ultimate act of anger.

I (Bridget) have also dealt with the families of those who have actually taken their lives. This is a very painful situation and leaves their loved ones in deep grief. They end up blaming themselves and never seem to get closure for this tragic loss.

If you feel that you have gotten to the "point of no return" and are preparing to take your life by detaching yourself from others, giving away your possessions, thinking there is nothing left to bring meaning into your life, etc. then do not sit on it or carry this burden alone. You must tell someone right away and get professional help immediately. Do not leave this serious situation to chance...it is nothing to play around with. Finding someone to share this with can give you a ray of hope in all your pain. It will lighten your burden and open up a new perspective to at least hang in there, knowing and believing that tomorrow is an opportunity to start a new day.

<u>Anxiety and nervousness</u>. An exaggerated startle response is set off by a variety of factors, such as: pop cans opening, fireworks, and other loud noises. Maybe these sounds jettison you into a state of combat readiness. Of course, the use of stimulants and some medications can also create an edge to our nervous system, so it is best to understand how your body responds to a state of anxiety. However, there is a time and place when medication may be necessary to relieve the symptoms of anxiety so you can sleep better and prevent you from getting over-stimulated by your environment. You can also do behavioral interventions that will aid in lowering your anxiety by doing something as simple as taking slow deep breaths or listening to soft music. In other words, feeding your inner person with soothing elements and becoming more aware of your body takes you out of a state of anxiety. This allows you to anchor yourself and feel more grounded in your surroundings. Finding a safe place in your

heart to create a sense of peace will do wonders to quiet the war that still rages within.

Another aspect of hyper arousal (hyper-vigilance) is being uncomfortable when people walk too closely behind you or sit near you in a confined space. After surviving months of guerilla or urban warfare, anxiety and nervousness are normal responses that contribute to generally making you feel suspicious of others. It is normal to feel this way after living beyond the normal range of human activities. It is also not unusual to find it difficult to trust others. I have heard veterans say that they sometimes feel like "crawling out of their skin" when immersed in crowds, public restaurants, or busy shopping malls.

The key to finding good coping for anxiety and nervousness is planning. Do what you can not to get caught off guard, or to put yourself into situations that will trigger your hyper-arousal unexpectedly.

Develop and practice foresight, just as you would if you were doing reconnaissance of an enemy-held territory. Look ahead, plan, and anticipate what could potentially occur. Ask yourself, Where will I be? Who I will I see? What will I be doing? How long will I stay? And how will I be able to make the best exit from the situation? Be careful not to let your anxiety get out of control by blowing a situation out of proportion. Get the facts straight and plan ahead, this will serve to reduce the fear factor which feeds anxiety.

In my practice (Bridget) one WWII veteran shared with me his simple, but creative, method of taking himself out of a situation when he felt anxiety coming on. He mentioned that whenever he was at social gatherings, public places, or even at a person's home he would excuse himself when his anxiety mounted. Even though he did not have a need to use the bathroom, he would find it a solitary and safe place that would allow him to take time out. He could catch his breath and calm himself down before returning to a social setting.

This was an excellent means of developing some positive self-care and coping skills. No one ever questions him or his reasons for leaving, nor do they even have an idea that his anxiety is spiraling out of control. He uses this to effectively manage his anxiety, and it works. Perhaps with a little work and creativity you too will be able to find what works best for you in these types of situations.

<u>Emotional constriction</u>. Is like putting all your emotions into a pressure cooker. Eventually the pressure can no longer be contained within your thoughts. Using the metaphor of "letting off a little steam" clearly takes on a more significant meaning. By letting off a little bit of steam (i.e., physical exercise, hobbies, dancing, traveling, etc.) you are gradually reducing the emotional pressure, therefore making these symptoms much more manageable and tolerable.

Talking about, and sharing, what is going on with you is an important way to also let off steam...it builds trust and intimacy in a relationship. However, it is easy to just brush aside, and say, "It don't mean nuthin'" like the

Vietnam veterans did, but in reality they too have developed an understanding that it is important to share their story and to have a witness to their emotional pain.

You will see by opening up a little at a time with a loved one, trusted friend, or a professional that this will ease the weight of carrying "it" all alone. "Humping" by yourself can be a lonely and difficult task, but when you reach out to a "buddy" the process suddenly becomes much more bearable. There is support around you, use it whenever you can to practice telling your story.

There are some things you will probably never share with another living soul. The things you do share have now changed you and made you into the man or woman you are today. Allow yourself to think for a moment what it would be like to begin the process of allowing someone "in" to a place you thought would be closed for all time. By denying yourself the opportunity to emote (feel) only sets you farther apart from your community and those who love you.

It is nearly impossible to achieve intimacy with your family, partner, or friends if you continue to hold back emotions because of fear. The fear is often times based on a false assumptions, or beliefs such as: "Once I start crying, I may never stop", "If I open myself up, I will go crazy", or "If my partner really knew what I did, they will reject me and I will no longer be loved". Rather than assuming the worst it is time to take the leap of faith and see how trust does go a long way towards developing a solid relationship. Let some pressure off and begin the process of feeling again; it is vital to survival and re-adjustment into your community.

One of the frustrating moments for veterans is when those who have never been to war ask, "What was it like?" or "Did you kill anybody?" (Yes, this happens more often than not.) As good as your intentions are to share experiences, and for those who ask to hear your story, it may be more difficult to do than you both think. They may not be prepared to hear the stark truth of the horrors and graphic details, so it is best to use caution and temper the words and descriptions you use to convey what you have seen and done. On the other hand, be prepared to deal with the reactions of those who ask these kinds of questions. They may catch you off guard. For example, the soldiers with whom I work have relayed to me many responses from people who have had their questions answered. It can be disheartening when they respond with, "You did that?" or "How could you have done such a thing?" Needless to say, this may be how a person will react to your answers. In doing so, little consideration is given to how their response will affect you. They just do not understand, and this will definitely be a chance for you to practice and exercise a new level of tolerance, and perhaps even forgiveness. They are unaware of your true feelings about your war-time duty and may be shocked to hear what you have to say. Remember, all they see is the person you were before you went to war, and now you are a different person and admitting to involvement in things that shock their senses.

Our topic here has been emotional constriction, and by no means are we advocating that should not talk about your experiences—we are only suggesting that you know your audience before opening up. Use discretion and good judgment. If you do, things will go better for you as you traverse the wire to come home.

Pass in Review

Reviewing some of these symptoms may have hit home for you. If what you have read has caused you some discomfort or uneasiness, then it may be wise to put our book down and come back to it when you are ready to continue. This is a common reaction. There is a lot of new information here and we do not want you to become overwhelmed. Remember you are not alone, and your reactions are normal, and we want you to hold onto this; so when times get tough remember that you are going to make it through this process. It does take time to absorb this and remember it is not about the destination, it is about the process.

However, we are hoping that the information has put you on a new course in understanding more about yourself and how your combat experiences have affected you. During your service time you have developed some useful coping skills of survival and self-awareness. Maybe you even look at life as something that is quite amazing, or perhaps you are feeling confused and angry about this whole thing. There can be a myriad of emotions and reactions that turn on while reviewing this information. We want you to evaluate how you are doing. If you feel you need extra support, reach out and find those who can provide more information and a safe place to talk. A good place to begin is the Veterans Administration Medical Centers and military support organizations such as your base community services. Don't attempt to do this alone; this requires a team effort and support. Just like any military operation...it cannot be done unless you have assistance from the rear.

Warning Signs of PTSD

Stress affects everyone differently. In most cases there are warning signs that indicate a need for active stress management:

Persistent fatigue
Inability to concentrate
Flashes of anger—lashing out at friends and family (or even yourself) for no apparent reason
Changes in eating and sleeping habits
Increased use of alcohol drugs, tobacco, etc.
Prolonged tension headaches, lower back aches, stomach problems or other physical problems
Prolonged feelings of depression, guilt, anxiety and helplessness

These are just some of the ways that PTSD may be affecting your life. The emotional and psychological stress of war does not go away simply by leaving it unattended. (That's the best way to stay outside the wire.) The symptoms need to be addressed, and you cannot do it alone.

Think of it this way...if you were wounded physically during combat you would allow a medic to attend to the wound. This is no different. Your psychological wounds must be attended to as well. They can be managed with proper help and support.

7.

Home. Really?

"Happy to be home? On one level, yes, but on another it's kind of a letdown. I get so bored most of the time that I'm always thinking of something to do that can get me up and going. The worst thing is driving. I'm looking toward the bridges and the overpasses all the time; looking at the sides of the roads and the guardrails. Driving is different now, and it's really strange to get stuck in traffic. No more hitting the gas pedal and jumping over curbs, speeding across highway medians or cutting off vehicles piled up at an intersection. In Iraq I could do whatever I wanted..."

—A Marine home from Iraq

Homecoming is a process, not a single event. It is one step at a time without expecting it to all go away. As soon as you set down in the USA it is easy to believe that your troubles are over, but don't get discouraged if life unravels around you. Remember...it is normal to think differently, and see life differently, after spending a year in a combat zone.

In making the transition from war to home the very first thing that combatants may notice is that they are on high alert most of the time. Hyper vigilance has become a part of life; it is what keeps one alive in war zones. Jumping at noises, unconsciously reaching for weapons, allowing anger to overpower, etc., can last for weeks, months, or even years after returning home.

You may expect it (stress reactions) to be gone in a month or so, but there are no guarantees that it will just naturally disappear. I (Chuck) expected many thoughts, behaviors, and habits to just go away when I got back from Vietnam, however most did not. Sadly, I suffered along with my loved ones for many long hard years afterwards. I found that these stress reactions do not go away by merely leaving them alone. They hide like snipers in the deep crevasses of our souls, and show up when least expected. I was getting ambushed.

As for the process, we must all remember that our lives are forever changed after war. There is no going back to square one to start over. We need not set an ambush for ourselves by thinking we can go back where we left off. It is important to re-frame our thoughts and notions of what life is like now.

As a returning combatant you will be different in some common situations. One Army wife said, "Not long after my husband came back from Iraq we took the kids to a circus. He was edgy being around the large crowd and noise. The moment a cannon was fired off as part of the show, he got up and left. He just up and walked out." If the wife did not know the mechanics of his stress, or expect this, she could take it personally. She could become upset to the point of adding more strain on their relationship.

As you can see these types of reactions can easily be misunderstood by those who were "not there". That is a perfect example of why it is important for both parties to be well informed about the various manifestations of stress reactions. For instance, if this wife had known that loud sounds such as a cannon exploding would have a triggered her husband, she could have warned him ahead of time. Or, perhaps, they may have even declined to attend such an event. Having this loving and understanding support from people with whom you associate, provides less of a burden for you to pack around.

Shaking It Off

People coming out of combat are usually in a hurry to get back home. Often times their first thought is "Let me get back home and get things back to normal. I need to shake this thing off."

I (Chuck) was in the worst rocket/mortar barrage of the entire Vietnam

War a couple of hours before getting on a plane to come home from 'Nam in 1966. (218 rockets fell on or near our position in less than an hour's time period). Every man in that little compound at the airbase was hit, and seven young men, who had spent a year humping rice paddies, died only hours before leaving for home. I was scratched up with small shrapnel wounds on my arms, but I wrapped them up and rolled my sleeves down. I decided not to go for treatment because I did not want to take the chance of being delayed in getting home. I am not an isolated case either...it was that way with many veterans. We know the same types of situations are happening with our troops coming home from the Global War on Terror.

Well, "shaking it off" works for awhile, but what you are taking lightly may come back to haunt you in the end. If you begin feeling detached from your feelings and thoughts, this may be a warning sign. You must remember that you are no longer in a military setting. It is time for you to consider reaching out for help.

It took me more than twenty years to admit that Vietnam had affected my life. In that time period I left a trail of broken marriages and families with much discord. From my perspective (and I'm sure Dr. Cantrell will concur) that this book is written in an effort to help you avoid some of the same pitfalls.

For years I did not want anything to do with the VA (thinking that only the guys who were physically wounded deserved treatment). I did not want to be a complainer; nor did I want anyone to know that something was wrong with me. My pride was working against me and I had no idea for many painful years. You do not have to let this be your story. Do not wait to address the issues you brought home.

To hide the effects of the war I drank and used plenty of drugs. I thought that if I acted out while being drunk or stoned people around me would merely think it was the substance I was on, and that my strange behavior had nothing to do with being in a war. I wanted to be a brave, whole person, and not a victim. I was an airborne soldier and knew I could suck it up, but it did not work. Secretly I was always alone...even in the middle of a crowd. I smiled on the outside, but wept on the inside. I used my social "camouflage" well. Fortunately, I did finally find meaning to my experiences. I then sought out professional help through the VA system and other veteran support groups like Point Man International. It has changed my life for the better.

***

The war goes on. Many Vietnam veterans have mentioned that they fully expected things to be the same when they got home. However, most have found that the war never ended; it only changed locales. Some have also stated that had they known that the battle for emotional wholeness would continue, they would have been more prepared and capable to deal with life.

Just as veterans from other eras have learned, some of those returning from Iraq and

Afghanistan begin battling with the first signs of post-traumatic stress almost immediately once they are home. Studies (Army Times 1/7/2005) have shown that the first signs of stress for many begin to appear 3 to 4 months after returning home. This can be attributed to the fact that you are experiencing difficulties re-adjusting to everyday life responsibilities. Your relationships may be crumbling or even failing, and the expectations of those around you are more demanding than you are able to handle. In other words, the difficulties with your re-adjustment can take time to surface. Once you realize that you have changed, and life demands are beckoning you, then the unraveling process can take on a life of its own.

In the spring of 2004, we (we called it the Dean/Cantrell Team) visited an Army Brigade in Italy. We went on an invitation from the U.S. Army. The particular unit was fresh out of combat in Iraq, and we noted that many of the personnel on post, from top to bottom, had an air of "caution" about them. These men and women had been exposed to sights, sounds, and smells on the battlefield that will stay with them forever.

An interesting observation worth noting is that most of them had heard of Post-Traumatic Stress Disorder (PTSD) from parents and grandparents of the Vietnam era. Some had seen first-hand the manifestations and/or problems that it can cause. Others had read and heard about PTSD, and knew what it looked like in real life...some had even witnessed the effects of trauma first-hand in their own homes growing up. This knowledge alone had caused some tenseness and a concern that they too may have "it". The fact is that many will have stress reactions related to their combat experiences, however, whether or not it develops into PTSD, only time will tell.

Life is different when you are no longer down range, and many of the survival skills you used in the war are not always appropriate in a civilian world. For example, you may feel more secure sleeping with a loaded weapon every night like you did in the combat zone. You may also respond differently now to stressful situations. You may find yourself ducking for cover when you hear loud noises (fireworks, automobile backfires, doors slamming, etc.). You may get nervous or anxious when you hear children playing, crying or screaming, as those sounds may have a negative memory associated with them with the combat zone. You have been trained and have become accustomed to situations that demand immediate action without hesitation or conscious thought. In other words, your response to environmental "triggers" is automatic with little thought to the consequences of your actions.

Now that you are home many of these particular ways of responding most likely are not conducive to a positive outcome. You are no longer in a situation where it is life or death, black or white, all or none. Choosing to find middle ground in life is never easy; however, it is worth every moment spent on the effort. In order to survive on the home front with your war-time past is now your challenge—and top priority. It is the foundational structure that transformation and re-integration rests upon.

The wise choices you make will assure a better outcome for you and those around you.

Something else to consider is that many changes have taken place at home while you were away. These changes can ignite a new fire and create a different set of stress factors for both you and your loved ones. For example, a person who leaves for nine months and has a 3-month-old child comes back to a toddler who can now walk and talk. You may have missed the first tooth and the first step, and the baby has no idea who you are.

The person you left at home, who once relied upon you, has become quite capable of managing the household by themselves. Many tasks you shared before your deployment, such as decision-making about children, household duties, finances and social activities, have now become the sole responsibilities of the person at home.

Perhaps it will be difficult to relinquish some of these duties. On the other hand, it may be that the person at home wants to "dump" everything back on you (the returning partner).

However, you may find that you are not emotionally available to accept these demands.

Careful consideration on both sides in reaching a successful balance in redistributing partnership responsibilities is vital in re-establishing a healthy union.

Time can also be a major factor: You may need much of your partner's time that had previously been allocated to others while you were away. Your partner may not be accustom to giving time and attention to you, and may now find that this demand is too much of an additional burden. Likewise, they may begin to resent you because your presence now represents an obstacle in their relationships. Now that you are home you could be considered a barrier that keeps them from spending as much time with their friends (i.e., support groups, etc.) whom they met during your absence. Relationships that were formed while you were away have a high probability of challenging your partnership.

There is hardly anything worse than a failed expectation for both the person arriving home and the person waiting for them to return. You both have your own ideas of what it will be like when you are re-united. Your dreams and hopes have been the fuel that has kept the anticipation of this reunification vibrant and alive. However, this anticipation can have negative effects on you, such as worry, fear, and anxiety. Both of you more than likely have developed different ideas, plans, and projections of what to expect on the homecoming.

These anticipated dreams of what you "expect" of your partner may create areas of contention. Compromise, flexibility and creativity will serve both of you well in finding middle ground in re-establishing your relationship.

Here's an interesting drill for you. It can be a very productive activity for noth you and your loved one(s). Make a list of the expectations that you have envisioned during your absence. Ask your partner to do the same. After you compile this list go over it and evaluate your realistic needs. Place a check mark indicating those expectations that are unreal and impossible to fulfill with your partner or existing family members. Once you have sorted out the unrealistic expectations, or those that seem too demanding, focus your attention on those that can be fulfilled. In other words, do what you can do, and avoid chewing off too much as you begin to work through this process.

Finally, it is important to first and foremost evaluate these expectations in union with your partner. Secondly, it is healthy knowing that you are not alone in dealing with the effects of war, and this can provide a special sense of confidence for you and your loved ones. Understanding and knowledge is always a powerful aspect in the healing process. Lastly, do not let unrealistic expectations "ambush" you in re-establishing harmony with your loved ones.

Yes, your life will be different after war and if you are aware of some of the key changes, your transition will be much smoother. You will be able to deal with the

Still Outside the Wire

"wire" much better. We hope these important aspects help as you traverse the wire on your way home.

Still Outside the Wire

8.

Outside the Wire Looking In

"The journey home marks the beginning of an internal war for the Marines. 'Give them the space they require to slowly turn the switch. The switch from violence to gentle. The switch from tension to relaxation. The switch from suspicion to trust. The switch from anger to peace. The switch from hate to love."
LT. Col. Mark Smith, WISHTV Feb.18, 2005

When you leave home to serve in the military you are stepping out of one world into another. In most cases you will be thrust into a new environment overnight where adapting and learning to survive with a new set of rules in unfamiliar surroundings is the order of the day. A new soldier (sailor, airmen, or marine) must strive to become a working member of this new life. In the process, one usually develops a new identity within this new "community" setting. You may even acquire a nickname and that is what defines you from that point on.

From day one of basic training, you begin to change, and it is the drill cadre's primary job to facilitate this metamorphosis. Combining this with the tremendous sense of personal danger and stress during wartime duty, it is easy for close family members to see how you have changed. Many of these changes can be alarming for unprepared family members. It is important to know that they probably will not get you back in the same state of mind in which you left. Not to say this is all bad, because you know that many of the changes in you can be attributed to a lot of personal growth.

Back on the Job

War veterans are impacted in ways that make it difficult to adjust and re-integrate back into the work place. These difficulties manifest themselves in various ways. It is common for them to feel that they cannot be around people, and many have problems with authority figures. On top of that, they may have a low frustration tolerance and no patience for simple mistakes by fellow workers (stupid decisions and mistakes could have gotten them killed "down range").

Because most jobs require contact with other people, and contain hierarchies of employees, veterans are easily reminded of many negative aspects of military life. Incompetent chains of command are just one pet peeve for most. Too many times inept combat leadership and poor decision-making resulted in life-threatening scenarios and people were needlessly wounded or killed. Veterans may easily bring this deadly reminder into a "normal" work place, and they may find themselves rebuffing directions or "orders" from a superior who has not proven to be a good decision maker.

As you can see, this is not conducive to maintaining job security. A work relationship like this can be detrimental and result in the veteran moving from job to job. Finally, they give up and remain unemployed. It is not uncommon to find veterans who have had dozens of jobs since returning from war. Not being able to achieve this viable level of productivity can affect one's self esteem and intimate relationships.

The inability to maintain relationships on the job has many additional destructive consequences. This can create stress on the family and marriage unit. (Financial security is of paramount importance in sustaining stable relationships. Providing for one's family is a very important aspect of feeling like a worthy and contributing partner.) This stability is often challenged when the veteran cannot maintain employment due to war wounds and/or stress.

Hard to Trust

Monty Bergsma, a close friend and veteran of Vietnam who became a wonderful artist after the war, spoke of some of his PTSD challenges. He told me if he did not distrust people then he would have to trust them. He went on to say that he just could not trust others because he was not ready to deal with being betrayed again. He then smiled and said, "My 'truster' is broken."

Trauma exposure clearly affects one's ability to discern, determine, or perhaps even have the desire to want a "normal" relationship. The relationships, which were formed while serving in the military, were based on the perspective and commitment that one would be willing to lay down their life for another person. It is all about trust and camaraderie.

Veterans have shared the deepest of human emotion, terror, vulnerability, hope, love and despair. They learned to bond based on these common emotions, and they formed connections that journey to the very depths of their souls. Consequently, the quality of these associations is unique and has not been able to be replicated in subsequent relationships since leaving the military. This is a major challenge in re-connecting with loved ones.

Inscribed on a "C" ration box by an unknown Marine at Khe Sahn, Vietnam in 1968 were these words. *"For those who fight for it, life has a special flavor the protected (will) never know"*. In these simple words emerge the very core of connection amongst veterans.

Your partner and family members may sense that you are unable to bond with them at a deep level. There is a time when loved ones feel as if their veteran is putting up a perimeter or a boundary, which does not let them in. Of course, this may be difficult for you to explain. You may even find yourself saying, "You weren't there, you don't understand".

You must understand the level of frustration family and partners go through by you having an unapproachable attitude. We encourage you to help them understand where you are coming from. We believe that a good place to begin is with agreements and commitments to better communication.

Keep in mind that your commitments require intent, desire, and a mutual vision to commit to another person. Trust is the most important element in this equation. In order to begin your journey in developing trust and commitment try this: Accept and practice the following agreements:

Agree to avoid (knowingly) hurting one another.
Agree to acknowledge the validity of the other person's viewpoint.
Agree to express empathy (understanding what it feels like to be in the other person's shoes).
Agree not to hide your feelings from one another (be vulnerable with each other).
Agree not to abandon each other in the face of the worst storms (be steadfast).
Agree to work out conflicts with each other (finding middle ground on issues).

Agree to take responsibility for your actions and make an effort to change in order to strengthen the relationship.

Agree to admit one's faults and wrong doings. Be quick to ask for forgiveness when you fall short of expectations.

Agree to acknowledge that you are starting from a new point in time—not from where you and your loved one were before they left for their military assignment.

9.

Asleep at the Wheel

"I could feel the darkness engulf my body, my will, and the very core of my spirit. The unbearable jungle heat wrapped around me and clung like a cellophane bag. I couldn't move; to move meant giving away my position, and "Charlie" was nearby because I could smell the fish on his breath. The dark was black; I couldn't see anything. The sweat pouring from my body was the only thing moving in the whole world. "What was that? Something close! Breathing! Yes, breathing, and it's on my face. It's time to go for it...it's him or me. Like a striking snake, both my hands shot straight out and clasped the scrawny, pathetic neck in front of me, and I

felt a gurgling deep in his throat as I applied pressure. I began to scream, "I'll kill you, I'll kill you!" "Suddenly, with a jerk, my prey wrenched free and was gone. The light came on, and I awoke to see my terror-stricken wife standing at our bedroom door gasping for air as she rubbed her throat where my hands had been seconds before."

—A night with a Combat Veteran

Many combat veterans stay awake as long as they possibly can. For them, sleep means another night back in combat. They are preparing for a night of patrols, breaking down doors and searching for weapons. They do this until daybreak; living every hour of darkness on complete alert and in terror of the unknown tactics used by an elusive enemy.

So what do you do? Perhaps you watch late night TV to occupy your attention. You drink jugs of coffee to stay awake and you drink alcohol to try to forget. You smoke to have something to do, and maybe you take pills to shut everything off. It becomes a ritual of "do anything other than fall asleep during the darkness". If you are going to sleep, you make sure the sun is up first. You may even find that after your spouse leaves the house to go to work you can finally relax—and maybe even sleep. With a sigh of relief, you stand down because now you are off duty. You see how this works? You were up all night (just like when you were down range) making sure that the "perimeter" was secure, and everyone in the house was safe.

Sleep disturbance is a common dilemma for combat veterans. The nightmares may center on a feeling of helplessness or re-enactments of past threats. Perhaps like running out of ammunition while still heavily engaged with enemy forces, or being a target for a roadside IED. The seriousness with sleep disturbance is that it brings about a multitude of other PTSD symptoms. Bodies and mental faculties are weakened and exhausted from fear, worry, and anxiety. We lose our built-in ability to rejuvenate through sleep when we are plagued with emotions such as these. With the lack of sleep we become wide-open to fatigue, poor attitudes, rage, intolerance, poor concentration, and depression. We can wear ourselves out. Our bodies will begin to signal us with simple messages through pain, numbness, fatigue, and even crankiness, just to name as few. So take heed and work on restoring the body and mind by addressing these vital issues.

Sometimes medication is the most effective means to get some relief from sleep deprivation...but we are not saying this is the only remedy. There are effective ways for you to be proactive in finding some relief on your own. Stress reducing exercises and activities, and a good diet can go a long way in helping you. Medication is certainly better than living from day to day burdened by lack of sleep, and can be a first line of defense for you. Do not take up a medicine regimen, however, without first consulting with a medical professional.

Our last bit of advice may seem simple, but we believe you need to know that it is okay to sleep whenever your body and mind tells you. It is perfectly fine to sleep day or night, and wherever you can...be it your bed, favorite chair, in your vehicle, or laying on the beach or front lawn...just do it!

Dread at Night, Fatigue by Day

Going to bed, or getting ready to, can bring about a heavy feeling of dread in you. It is not much different from the feeling just before going out on patrol. The unpleasantness of the filthy environment, coupled with the threat of someone waiting in ambush to kill all comes back frequently in the form of dreams. Once sleep comes, past experiences can be re-lived perhaps by such events as the recent death of a friend, getting separated from buddies while going house-to-house, being hit in a Humvee with an RPG or IED, or seeing bodies being torn apart by shrapnel.

Even though it disturbs your rest, sleep disturbance has its most harmful effects during waking hours. Nightmares, whether or not you have been in combat, can leave lasting impressions throughout the next day. Many people have reported terrible headaches as a result of a dream the night before. The nightmares tend to be inconclusive, and unresolved, and one can sense they are not really "over". So veterans subconsciously work throughout the day to bring these experiences to some kind of resolution and conclusion. As easily imagined, the repercussions of having a terrible dream every time you close your eyes could be overwhelming. It makes both night and day an unreal world of terror, ready to strike at any time.

An impacting side-effect is that spouses of veterans also suffer from their mates' sleep disturbances. Some complain about being frightened as their loved ones shout out commands and cries of terror while asleep. A more serious fear is of actual bodily harm. The partner does not know when the dreaming mate may be "triggered" into a combat mode that might be life threatening. A consequence of your sleep patterns, which may be violent, is that your partner, who has never been to war, may also begin to practice a form of hyper-vigilance. This can be a result of the fear of being harmed by you in the middle of the night.

Simple solutions to this situation is agree to sleep separately for as long as needed, and remove all weapons or threatening implements from your environment.

A Mixed-Up "Time Path"

Tension and anxiety have tendency to sneak up on us when we are feeling vulnerable and can wreak havoc with our lives. Fears, real or imagined, are oftentimes the underpinnings of stress. These fears may be very real, and are associated with mental images on our "time path". Everyone has a mental recording of everything he or she has ever experienced. On this time path we have real fears of near-death/near-pain situations of while we were down range. These situations return to the present in the form of nightmares, intrusive thoughts and behaviors, accompanied with complete scenery and events as we saw or felt them during the incident(s).

On a daily basis we attempt to sort through the items recorded on our mental files just to make sense of our lives. We find that certain high impact events, feelings, and situations stand out and shape our attitudes and senses, and sometimes dictate to us the way we ought to see and react to life. For example, most of us view life differently than we did before we watched the planes crash into the Twin Towers on 9/11. We have mental pictures that will be with us for the rest of our lives. Nightmares are related to events from the past and they are based on past experiences and are no longer considered a present-time threat.

Our "time path" can get out of order by trauma. The threat of imminent danger for self and others, and the near loss of life and/or limb, can become so great the images reel off as if the events were taking place in the present. When we let our minds go to these traumatic pictures certain responses can overtake us by a myriad of perplexing, and sometimes unwanted, emotional responses.

To Sleep is to Give Up Control

It is tough to sleep. When we go to sleep, we feel more vulnerable and a loss of control. It may be scary to find that we are no longer in charge of our "area", and sleeping puts us in a place of defenseless against any outside forces, which may appear in the form of these mental images. The feelings and thoughts we associate with these impressions disturb and interrupt our rest.

Many times our mental pictures can be similar or variations of a recurring theme. As with any traumatic experience, these images are lodged in portions of our mind that are not fully available to us on a conscience level. When we sleep, we do not have the defense mechanisms in place to guard against these intrusive thoughts or images. Consequently, very little of the full content in these dream states remains with us, but enough is there so that it has an adverse affect on our lives.

We are "vulnerable" while we sleep. That is why many of us stay awake as long as we possibly can. "Awake" equals control – "Sleep" equals no control. The irony is that by attempting to maintain control of the night (staying awake), we begin to lose control of our waking world. Our bodies were made to recuperate through rest.

Since dreams have a way of discharging mental energy, they become "work" and cause fatigue for many veterans struggling with PTSD. We wake up feeling exhausted instead of rested.

Here are a couple of ways you can help yourself regarding your sleep disturbance and nightmares:

First and most importantly, do not hesitate to seek professional medical help. Go to a doctor who can evaluate your condition and give you competent, professional suggestions. In some cases, medication may be necessary to help you "cool down" (or rest up) before you try anything else.

Recognize that your mental and physical time paths do not coincide. One of the best things you can do is to talk about the "then" and the "now" with another trusted person. A sensitive person can help you see and accept that you are probably not in any present danger. Begin to make clear distinctions between past experience and present reality. (Understand as well that a flashback is really a bad case of being thrown out of the present time, and a warrior can get stuck in those past mental images which prohibit him or her from living in the present.)

It is important to remain aware of the importance of sleep in your recovery process. Sleep is one of the most fundamental requirements for good health both physically and mentally. It is vital in making back across the wire in good order.

Still Outside the Wire

10.

Guilt ... An Adhesive Element

Guilt deserves its own chapter in any book about PTSD. It is elusive, and one of the main adhesive elements in keeping warriors outside the wire. It can have negative or positive features that are borne from our life experiences. In something as chaotic as war there are plenty of opportunities to live in a situation that lends itself for you to come away with a strong sense of guilt.

First of all, there is a positive characteristic to guilt. Without it humans would be void of a sense of remorse if they did not feel bad about causing harm or destruction. We can all be thankful for this type of guilt because it can serve to inhibit a continuum of bad stuff in our world. Feeling bad and taking action to remedy unpleasant consequences is a good thing.

Negative guilt, however, can enslave us unnecessarily to many severe PTSD symptoms. The misery of being shackled to memories laced with guilt is a prison that we impose upon ourselves. If these memories are left unaddressed, they will only worsen with time.

"Why did I live when other people died?" "I should have died, and they should have lived." "It should have been me instead."

These are some expressions of survivor guilt. This type of guilt is a way to make sense, or justify why you are the one sitting here reading this book and perhaps your deceased friend is not.

As survivors, we tend to want to trade places with the person who died. Time and time again, we have heard veterans say that the guys who died were the lucky ones, because they do not have to be around to suffer the pain and agony of shame, flashbacks, depression, or nightmares.

You may go through varying mood swings carrying this type of guilt. We can experience a lot of self-doubt, and set out to punish ourselves for surviving when others more "worthy" died during combat.

As survivors, we can go from being quite normal to a low state of depression, then swing into a high state of hyper alertness and anxiety in a matter of minutes; especially if our life situation becomes tumultuous. Tensions in our daily life, such as marital stress, employment difficulties, poor health, and financial worries can trigger these stressors.

The Impulse to Self-Destruct

Many who are challenged with survivor guilt lead interesting "flash-pan" lives. By this we mean that some veterans may travel a precarious path and even seem to look for the biggest guy in the bar to fight, knowing full well they may lose or go to jail. It is difficult to ascertain exactly how many veterans have taken their own lives in what appeared to be a single-motor vehicle accident. On the other hand, some veterans may feel that they have to "give" all their time and energy away. Others become compulsive blood donors and find considerable relief in giving their blood so others can live.

Guilt is an emotional reaction resulting from an event or behavior that perceives as wrong. Breaking a law or an agreement can send this emotional response into action. Some indicators of guilt are depression, self-punishment, low self-esteem, headaches, chronic fatigue, constant criticism of others, and fear of setting out on new tasks because you think you are incompetent or a failure. Developing relationships can be most challenging, in that you may feel you are not worthy of loving or being loved in the wake of your guilt.

Many have gone to a war zone trained to kill the enemy, but few were mentally prepared for the reality of that action. I do not remember ever being trained to psychologically withstand the shock of taking a life or losing a close friend in war. Sometimes I feel the military expect soldiers to walk through the fire without ever getting burned, but those memories that are forever seared in the mind are impossible to avoid. If only there was a silver bullet...a magical antidote...that could un-train warriors to not kill or fight on impulse as they are trained to do.

Shame

One of the most upsetting events that can take place is for someone to openly and unjustly accuse a veteran of doing something wrong. This has devastating effects on someone who feels they deserve more from a society, or people, they were willing to endure hardships for.

Shame actually triggers veterans into questioning and belittling themselves. It can also produce a great deal of resentment towards the accuser and a self-loathing for the person feeling shameful. The guilt produced by shame and unfounded accusations may lead to frustration and possibly a number of antisocial behaviors and PTSD symptoms.

If shame is left unattended, it festers. The guilt a veteran experiences through shame can cause a feeling of being "used up", and they may become lethargic about life and depressed. It can take a considerable push to get them to move freely on their own initiative. Like a heavily laden backpack, shame and guilt can sap one's vitality for life.

Medical Personnel and Guilt

Medical personnel, who get sent into combat to patch up the wounded and save lives on the battlefield often suffer the most painful symptoms of guilt. They were trained for a few months, and sent to a unit to become the "Doc." With a limited amount of medical knowledge, they perform courageously and save many lives. Some of the troops they administer their new skills to however, do not make it on the battlefield. Many wounded are beyond all medical help and die, much to the dismay of the medic attending them. Consequently, medics and corpsman harbor a great deal of pain and guilt due to a feeling of "incompetence" of not being able to save lives. For these brave men and women, who do their best with what they have, the hurtful memories impact them deeply. Many come home blaming themselves for others' deaths or pain.

Some military medical personnel admit guilt because they develop a dislike for the indigenous people in a war zone where guerilla warfare is being fought. Since it is difficult to identify the enemy, no one, including medical personnel, really knows who is responsible for all the terrible wounds they encounter on a daily basis. When asked to treat wounded Iraqis or Afghanis, many of these medics now live with the guilt of having had less than compassionate feelings for enemy casualties.

The medical corps working in triage and field hospitals have their own set of trauma experiences. Many troops, who should have been killed, were evacuated and brought to them for emergency medical attention. They saw soldiers and civilians (who would have easily died in previous wars) live and suffer on their operating tables. Troops with severe amputations, burns, and multiple fragment wounds are living to tell these medics about the horrors of their battles. In past wars, soldiers in these conditions would have been quickly stuffed into body bags and sent home. The medical personnel never would have seen them. In modern war, however, the advancement of medical technology and speed of evacuation methods are keeping more combatants alive than ever before.

As a case in point, I have a friend who served as a nurse at the 93d Field Evacuation Hospital at Long Binh, Vietnam in the late 60's. She was one of the nurses who patched up my unit after it nearly got wiped out on Hill 875 at Dak To. (She was in the Pleiku area at the time.) Our own planes dropped 500-pound bombs on the 173d Airborne (by mistake) while it was engaged in heavy fighting to take the hill, and the casualty numbers were off the chart.

During the course of the action and confusion, she had the ghastly job of tending to the exhausted and wounded paratroopers who had survived. They brought the wounded down in helicopters and the dead in dump trucks. My nurse friend tells me there was one thing about the whole episode that sticks in her mind. In her words, "All the bodies were already rotting...the dead and the living."

She is doing better today, but for years she has lived with inexpressible grief, heartache, and guilt. Fortunately, she has found a way and some good friends to help her recover from most of her war-caused problems.

Super Survivors

Many super-active "survivors" use adrenaline for medication. Many take high risks in occupations or recreational sports such as rock climbing, parachuting, or racing cars and motorcycles. Some find exciting relief through torrential sexual encounters with many partners.

As you can easily imagine, living with a combat veteran who suffers from survivor guilt can be a harrowing experience. It is not easy trying to keep up with someone who is running so fast, as to blot out the mental images of past terror, pain, and a feeling of unworthiness. It is a job in itself trying to pin them down long enough to administer help.

Connecting in relationships is particularly difficult with these super survivors. If you believe that you are an "adrenaline junkie", as some veterans are referred to, we strongly advise that you consider your position. It is not to your advantage to continuously feed this part of your psychological wounding. For some of you, your obsession for the rush of adrenaline may be a way to feed your ego. It can even give you cause to brag about your high risk behaviors, which can be an excuse for not "feeling" what is authentic or real.

For others, the addiction to adrenaline that served as a necessary survival tool in the combat zone may now be used as fuel to engage you in workaholic behaviors. Working two or three jobs, long demanding work hours, and filling job requirements that are extreme to the general public, may be a form of denial and a method of distracting you from a painful past. Absorbing yourself in work commitments to the point of forsaking all other responsibilities is not conducive to successful relationships, or a productive re-adjustment. One ER nurse, who had been a nurse in the war and is now working in an emergency room stateside, continues to feed her drive for adrenaline by working many overtime hours each day. She admits, "It's how I know I am still alive, otherwise I would just be numb and not care about life".

Considering all this, and doing all things in moderation, is important to your survival now that you are home. It is our hope that you take time to listen when someone suggests that you are out of control, do not just blow them off. Re-evaluate what is truly important for the good of your life and those with whom you associate and love.

Still Outside the Wire

11.

Not Home Alone

Very rarely are warriors called up to conduct solo operations; it is nearly always a team effort. However, in so many cases of veterans struggling to make some peace with returning home, to what feels like an alien environment, we find ourselves alone and believing that no one else in the world has experienced what we did. As I (Chuck) mentioned earlier, when I found out that there were others that had similar paths I discovered it to be an invaluable tool in help me find some relief, and a bit of healing I never expected.

The next section is included to illustrate that you are not alone with your feelings and experiences. Over the years we have collected many vignettes of comments and accounts of veterans from many eras and countries. When you read these you will see how much we all have in common, and how many there are of us. We believe that for this to be included it will help you find a bit of solace, and hopefully a sigh of relief that you are not alone in all of this.

Russia, Afghanistan

"When I came back, I began to scream at night in my sleep. During the war I drove over an American-made mine that is what put me in the hospital. American weapons killed my friends that the Mujahedeen used against us, and for a long time I was very angry at all Americans. I had lost my leg and thought my life was over. I drank and drank just to ease the pain.

I had this friend after the war. He too was a soldier in Afghanistan. He really was able to help me stop drinking. And because he cared and knew what I had gone through, he listened and heard me; therefore he was able to help me. Then eighteen months ago he died from the wounds he brought back from the war, and I began to drink again.

Five of us served together, but only two of us came home alive. Now that Pasha is gone there are only my memories...memories that I can't wash away no matter how much alcohol I drink."

Argentina, Falkland Islands.

"From the start, we were cold and wet in the inadequate clothing they had issued us. Most of us had been sent from Argentina's poor northern regions to fight the British on the Malvinas Islands, (Falklands). We were from the northern region that has a near-tropical climate and were ill-prepared for the damp and cold. Untrained and hungry (because the supplies sent to us never arrived,) we were completely confused.

The year was 1982, and now there are about 10,000 of us Malvinas war veterans left. I believe that the world looks at ours as a "silly little war," but I still remember it as a hell of futility. We were outgunned, outmaneuvered, and our losses caused our country to suffer a humiliating defeat. Now we veterans of that war are nothing more than an unpleasant reminder of our country's disgrace.

After the war the government promised us jobs, educations, subsidies, and a smooth transition back into society. But none of that materialized for us. Every time I go out looking for a job now and I tell them that I am a veteran of Malvinas, and they see me as wild, unstable, and undesirable. The people of Argentina do not like to think about us very much, because they see us as mirrors of the corruption in all of us. I believe we are all under a curse of guilt, but the soldiers are the obvious ones to blame.

My friends who were wounded got some initial medical attention, but now get only a little follow up care. Many of our soldiers died down there, and someone told me that they are building a memorial monument to them in La Plata. They can recognize the dead, but what about us who are still alive?

When our country decided to take the Islands back from Britain, they sent us, (mostly 18 and 19 year olds), to do the fighting. We had practically no training, and some of us had only fired a few rounds from our weapons in preparation. We were no match for the British. Our return home was not a victorious one at all, and now I often wonder if life is worth living. Suicide seems to be the best way out of this hell I live day after day."

U.S.A. WWII

Twenty-two years after his last combat experience in World War II, America's best known hero, Audie Murphy, still slept with the lights on and a loaded .45 caliber pistol by his bed. The only problem is, he couldn't bring himself to ask for help concerning his war stress, after all, he had won The Congressional Medal of Honor.

Still Outside the Wire

The World War II generation—we were a tough, uncomplaining people and children of the Depression generation. We were sent off to war in 1941 to wage a victorious defense of freedom and humanity. We were irrepressible in our pursuit of the American Dream, and entered the combat theaters with a sense of honor and glory that the world had never seen before.

My unit had its baptism of fire in North Africa. I survived 39 months of sustained combat, and never got hit. Coming home I went back to work at the plant but things weren't right. At night I was having severe "battle dreams," and in the daytime I would go through periods of partial amnesia; I couldn't even remember my own name.

Since I didn't get wounded I kept my mouth shut about these things, figuring that only the guys who got hit had any problems. Besides, it wasn't too popular to admit that the war had caused any mental problems. I wanted to fit back in and be normal again so I joined a veterans club, not so much for the friendship, but for the opportunity to drink my problems away in the familiar environment of soldiers.

There were times when I knew that I was out of control, and I would have to take time off work. I was staying up all hours of the night, afraid to go to sleep because of that same dream I kept having. By daybreak I would be so exhausted that I couldn't even get in my car to drive.

During my days off I retreated to my own little "foxhole," a small, dimly lit room that was filled with some old relics I brought home from the war. There I would spend time with my demons, and they would torment my mind through the memories of what I had seen and experienced in Africa. Nobody at work ever knew of my problems because I covered it up so well. I never wanted anyone to think I was crazy because of the war."

U.S.A., Korea

In November we moved within about ten miles of the Yalu River, right at the top of Korea. I was on a forward observers post and saw thousands of enemy soldiers fill the valley below.

As I reported the figures to the command over the field telephone, they refused to believe me. "Yes," I said, "thousands, sir!" Frustrated, I slammed the phone down and watched in horror as the sea of life moved straight for us. The enemy forces wanted the Yalu real bad. They pushed us back, slaughtered us, and that bit of war was one of the worst defeats in history. We kept falling back and regrouping, and each time we regrouped, the group was smaller. We had no choice but to fall back because we had no reinforcements or re-supply. It wasn't like when I fought in Vietnam years later; we couldn't call in artillery or air strikes at the drop of a hat.

Still Outside the Wire

We were just out there to face the human wave charges with what guts we had, and the little bit of weaponry that we could pack on our backs. Ultimately I was alone and became lost from my friends. Armed only with an Ml Garand rifle and a few clips of ammo, I evaded the enemy for three days, trying to get back to our lines. There was only snow, ice, slush, mud, cold and terror, as I made my way carefully past all the thousands of enemy troops that permeated the frozen hillsides.

Even though we got a few parades when we arrived back to the States. America wasn't sure if the war was over or not, and it just sort of wound down with nothing to end it except a "cease-fire," with neither side winning. We soldiers knew that we had fought hard, but since there was no victory and just a stalemate, we became a part of America that was put on hold to see "what would happen next" in Korea.

I was discharged and went silently back to my job. I was as confused as everyone else about the "police action," and not much was mentioned about it after that. At times I would feel some bitterness begin to rise up inside me about the war, and how we soldiers were ignored for our efforts. The best way for me to control any bad feelings and resentments was to work hard in the days and drink a lot at night. My wife and I became regulars at several taverns and dance halls, but my drinking became a threat to our marriage. When I would get drunk I would either become remorseful or belligerent. I would end up crying in my beer, or pick out the biggest drunk in the place and call him outside to fight. I just had too much pent up frustrations that I had to release it somehow."

Sweden, Africa UN

"In 1970 I left Sweden for duty in the Congo. I was excited to be a part of the United Nations Peace Keeping Forces sent there to end the revolution and civil war. And as a combat photographer I was always where the most action was. There was much killing while

we were there. Brother killing brother over political issues that were centuries old.

Arriving at Katanga I witnessed one of war's horrible impacts. I saw over 60,000 refugees, mostly women and children, in flight for their lives. The "Balubas" (the rebel faction) had caused much terror and the people were seeking safety at the edge of raging battles.

One day a Swedish commanding officer ordered us to transport some of these refugees on a train. We were to take them through dangerous territory; there were approximately 10,000 Balubas on patrol in the area. It was during this trip that I met a Belgium man who offered me 91 some very nice cameras to help me do my job. We made arrangements to meet the next day at a designated point of rendezvous.

The following day I arrived but the Belgium wasn't there. Instead I found all the cameras broken and smashed on the floor of the house. I felt that something must have gone wrong, so I carefully stepped back outside to be confronted by five men. One had a rifle and the others were armed with long knives. Immediately I dropped to the ground and they began to fire at me. I shot three of them in the faces and chest with my weapon on full automatic, but the remaining two tried to run away. I knew that if I allowed any to escape they would bring back more to help them kill or capture me—I determined not to let them get away. As they turned to run I shot both of them in the back and killed them immediately.

After the brief fight I went to the two that I had shot in the back and turned them over. I was shocked to see that they were boys, perhaps ten years old, and not soldiers. I began to throw up from the sickness that had come over me. As I heaved my insides out I looked down at the blue beret that I was clutching in my right hand; all I could think of when I saw that United Nations symbol of peace pinned to it was, "I failed my mission to come to the Congo as a peacekeeper. I had made a grave mistake." I didn't tell anyone about that incident, and kept it to myself.

I stayed 14 months in the Congo, and two days before I was to leave for my home in Sweden I was captured by the Katanga Forces and held for forty-four more days. This was my farewell party from Africa.

I thought that after I was released and I returned to Sweden that my problems would be over, but by then I had turned into a chain smoker because I was a nervous wreck, and my drinking of alcohol was elevated to disastrous proportions. I couldn't find peace no matter what I did.

I was a hero at home for my duty in Africa, but I was being eaten alive on the inside from guilt. Three times I've tried to commit suicide but failed. Now I dream about my time in the Congo, and I see the faces of those young African boys and they are always tattooed across my vision."

French-Indochina War

"In any war there are many important battles...some more so than others. But to the soldier he battles he fights in and lives through are always the most significant. The battle to clear An Khe in the central highlands of Vietnam on January 24, 1952 was said to be an historical one—this was my battle of all battles.

Early on the 24th of January my company, members of the elite French Battalion Parachutists Vietnam, executed a parachute assault landing into the area of Pleiku. From there we immediately made a forced march north to An Khe. There we engaged a reinforced battalion of the 302nd Viet Minh Division.

I was the officer in charge of 129 parachutists. As we entered the hamlet of An Khe we encountered heavy enemy resistance. Soon after assaulting the enemy positions we realized that we had walked into a major ambush, and the Viet Minh's horseshoe shaped ambush quickly encircled us.

It was living hell, but there was not time for fear and second thoughts. As a combat leader I immediately assessed our situation and ordered my men to assault the enemy lines to the west. I knew that if we could break through their lines in that direction we would have a good chance of making it to the security of friendly reinforcements at Quang Tri. After much hard fighting we broke through the ambush and made our way to safety in the west. Of the 129 soldiers I started with under my command only 70 made it out alive.

I went on to retire as a Colonel in the French army, but to this day I can never forget the battle of An Khe. Nor can I forget the faces of the brave men who followed me that day. I'm thankful for the ones who live, yet sad for the 59 who didn't. Sometimes I wonder if perhaps I'd done something different they may still be alive."

Still Outside the Wire

12.

Finding a Safe Outlet

A good place to begin dealing with the wire is to disclose your "wire" to trusted friends and loved ones. Let them know that it is there...and why it exists. They don't know it's there, but sure would like to know about it, and they cannot read your mind. (It may be appropriate to apologize for making them feel unwanted or pushed away at times in the past.)

In the beginning of this book we spoke of a GWOT trooper that we met in Italy that had a problem with his kids being too rowdy and when he couldn't take it any longer he would return to the military base to be with his buddies. When we told him about the "wire" and how he was most likely on the other side looking in he seemed to brighten up and get some understanding that he previously was unaware of. He needed to get this understand about the wire. He truly valued the insight on how the wire mechanism had affected his life. It began to normalize his experience a bit more. What he needed to hear more than anything else is how normal it was for him to react this way. It was a normal response for someone who had experienced what he had over the past several months. Just to know that he was not alone in his feelings, and that others struggle in similar ways, attributed to a very cathartic moment for him.

As an encouragement for you, make a conscious effort to allow loved ones to pass over to the other side of your "wire" once in awhile. This will work as long as you maintain control...and go slow with it. It is not advisable to allow anyone else the freedom to dictate the pace in this process; you know better than anyone what your tolerance level is with something like this. Agree with your friends and family that this process requires give and take, and for them not to take it personally but if you "kindly" suggest that they back off and allow you to re-set your perimeter things will go smoothly. The more mindful efforts you practice, the more successful it will be. Hopefully it will become a healthy exercise for everyone involved.

***

One main reason warriors prefer staying outside the wire when they come home is because of the hassle involved in trying to get back to normal civilian life. Most vets I know just don't want to get into why they stay disconnected.

Stuffing memories to hold back feelings of pain and despair is not a good thing. The "stuffing", however, becomes a full-time job once we come home from war. We can only hold such things inside for a short while before they begin to explode. When they do start to go off it may be when we least expect it, and are not in control of our faculties. The worst part of this is that not being in control is a trigger and a very daunting phenomenon for most combat veterans.

Like physical wounds, psychological and emotional wounds need to be cleansed before they can heal. These kinds of wounds are best purified by systematically dumping. Letting it out by talking about (cognitive therapy) the hurt, anger, sorrow, terror, and remorse a bit at a time is the best method. It is much like a pressure cooker with an outlet valve that regulates your release.

Living with the veil of guilt as we have said before is a heavy burden to carry. Your recovery from the guilt (especially caused by surviving when someone else did not) begins when you can separate out the responsibilities in the incident. Proactively direct yourself to think it through. Face your grief squarely, and separate out what is real from your irrational beliefs. You may actually have to list the facts about certain incidents on paper in order to determine what you actually believe about them. This will give a more clear perspective of what really went down. A good idea is to discuss the incident with others who were there with you if at all possible. This too can substantiate the real facts and give you some relief.

Once you see what is true about each situation, according to the facts, you will begin to discover both positive and negative guilt. If it is negative, it is something that needs to be dealt with. Often you will recognize that the death of someone else had very little to do with whether you lived or died. This task of "sorting out" can bring you to the point of taking responsibility for your past (and present) actions, while at the same time allowing you to freely feel emotions of sadness, anguish, and grief as part of the healing process.

The second simple release from this form of guilt is to know that it is okay to feel sad about the person who died in the incident, and is okay to cry and process through a legitimate time of grieving. It is, however, equally as important to know that dwelling on the incident(s) for excessive periods of time does little to help either. If you find you cannot move forward, it is advisable to schedule an appointment with a professional.

The third release you can give yourself is to realize that your survival does not make you responsible for their deaths. If you have to blame something for losing your friends, blame the war, not yourself.

Perhaps the most important resource you can use to bind up some of these wounds, and begin to heal them, is to seek out another combat veteran (who is healthy enough to be a safe sounding board) and unload the entire incident. Keep unloading. It is very important to tell the whole story, not just parts of it. Tell as many details as possible. Remembering such things as smells, noises, and perhaps the type of clothing you were wearing. Think back to the other environmental conditions that can guide you into a more precise recollection. Going over your story many times will help you remember more things. As you repeat the re-telling of the experience you will find a growing confidence to open up and tell more.

Recognize that you will probably experience sudden bursts of grief during these story-telling times. It is okay to let it all go. Nobody has ever died from crying. Once you get it out, you will feel much better. When you have detailed your entire story to an understanding "listener," you will find the healing process heading in the right direction.

The catch is that veterans do not find many "safe" people to talk to about their experiences, and that is why veterans-for-veterans groups are good. (We must not ignore the fact that there are many non-veteran professionals in the mental health field who are experienced in dealing with veteran issues and war trauma. Their compassion and professionalism definitely make them "safe" communication outlets. For years I personally found my group at the VA Medical Center very beneficial.)

During the years of work with Point Man International I (Chuck) have also been privileged to see many lives be changed and made stronger through their group meetings. It is encouraging now to see many new outreaches availing themselves to veterans and their families. There are veterans-for-veterans support groups around the country now doing similar work, and we recommend that you look into what they have to offer.

So what are these groups like? To begin with, the purpose of these groups is to provide a safe environment so you can feel comfortable and accepted; accepted in the company of those with similar military experiences. It is a place where you can freely express yourself and be understood. A place where it is safe to talk about the horrible things you witnessed, did, or failed to do while deployed. And most importantly, it is a place where no one will judge you. This is a great beginning to cleanse the wounds you may be carrying in your heart—wounds that keep you outside the wire.

A large part of coming home is relating to veterans of all eras...or even other countries; perhaps your one-time enemy. Getting to know one another and relating experiences can be tremendously healing. We encourage you to embrace other veterans and find time to associate with them. Therefore, let us not squander all those hard-learned lessons. Veterans should work together now to help shorten the time period for all soldiers like you, by sharing their knowledge and helping you sort out the stressful reactions to the war you were in.

"In the past, professionals did not really understand the effects of trauma on combat troops to the extent they do today. Thanks to the Vietnam era veterans who stood up and challenged the institutionalized thinking, we now have a tremendous base of knowledge from which to work." (T. Schumacher, personal communication, January 25, 2005)

We know that battle-hardened soldiers are reluctant to talk about their issues. Some of this is because of the risk they take in admitting a problem when it may reflect poorly on their records. If the soldier plans on making a career of the military, this could present a threat of not being advanced in rank. One bastion of confidence that remains in the military is the chaplain corps. Troops generally feel more open to discussing their PTSD issues with a chaplain, not only because of the confidentiality, but because of the non-threatening nature and appearance of spiritual counseling.

The good news, however, is that with the realization that the clinical programs at the VA to address PTSD were designed for veterans primarily of past wars, new programs are now in place for contemporary combatants. GWOT troops can get access to vet-to-vet support groups, individual mental-health therapy and treatment (for such problems as nightmares, sleeplessness, depression, anxiety, unexplained anger, and the other stress disorders) through a variety of providers. The VA Medical Center PTSD programs that offer counseling can be found across the country and many territories. For vet-to-vet support Veterans Outreach Centers are located nationally as well. Point Man International is one veteran-for-veteran organization that offers group and individual services as well (800-877-VETS).

The Army One Source hotline (800-464-8107) offers warriors and their families' 24-hour confidential consultation and referral seven days a week, as well as free, private, in-person counseling sessions in local communities.

A Parting Shot

It is important to fully understand that there are many circumstances in which we have little control, and these circumstances arise frequently while engaged in a war zone. This is why it is imperative to understand what "normal responses" to uncontrollable or abnormal circumstances are...they are just that...*normal*. These responses provide us with defenses against hard-hitting and debilitating reactions when direct control is not possible. In war it is difficult (nearly impossible) to control pain, fear, grief, death, and the myriad of other human reactions in the experience. As a veteran you should fully understand that it is normal not to have been in control of many circumstances during your service. What is happening is not out of the ordinary for you and many of your comrades-in-arms.

It is our hope that you successfully find your way back inside the wire. The world needs you.

The Authors

A Note to those who love veterans:

It's a weird thing...veterans can get addicted to war. Although he loves you it's hard for him to be 100% there when his attention is stuck somewhere on a battlefield. War is horrible, but there is nothing like a life-and-death fight to make you feel truly alive. The adrenaline rush is tremendous, and can never be replaced. Succeeding in combat defines a warrior, places him in a brotherhood where he is always welcome and understood. He just wants you to understand a little of where he's been. And remember; don't take it personal because he does love you.

Top Ten Things Your Combat Vets Want You to Know

By *Dr. Regina Bahten

"I'm a psychiatrist. Every day I listen to my combat veterans as they struggle to return to the "normal" world after having a deeply life-changing experience. I do everything I can to help them. Sometimes that can involve medications, but listening is the key. Sometimes a combat veteran tells me things that they wish their families knew. They have asked me to write something for their families, from my unique position as soldier, wife, and physician. These are generalizations; not all veterans have these reactions, but they are the concerns most commonly shared with me."

(Author's note: obviously warriors can be female — like me — and family can be male, but for clarity's sake I will write assuming a male soldier and female family.)

The List:

1. He is addicted to war although he loves you. War is horrible, but there is nothing like a life-and-death fight to make you feel truly alive. The adrenaline rush is tremendous, and can never be replaced. Succeeding in combat defines a warrior, places him in a brotherhood where he is always welcome and understood. The civilian world has its adrenaline junkies as well; just ask any retired firefighter, police officer, or emergency room staff if they miss it.

2. Living for you is harder. It would be easy for him to die for you because he loves you. Living for you, which is what you actually want, is harder for him. It is even harder for him if you are smart and do not need him to rescue you, since rescuing is something he does really well. If you are very competent at many things, he may at times question if you need him at all. He may not see that you stay with him as a conscious choice.

3. "The training kicks in" means something very different to him. It is direct battle doctrine that when ambushed by a superior force, the correct response is "Apply maximum firepower and break contact." A warrior has to be able to respond to threat with minimal time pondering choices. While this is life-saving in combat, it is not helpful in the much slower-paced civilian world. A better rule in the civilian world would be to give a reaction proportionate to the provocation. Small provocation, small response (but this could get you killed on the battlefield). When the training becomes second nature, a warrior might take any adrenaline rush as a cue to "apply maximum firepower." This can become particularly unfortunate if someone starts to cry. Tears are unbearable to him; they create explosive emotions in him that are difficult for him to control. Unfortunately, that can lead to a warrior responding to strong waves of guilt by applying more "maximum firepower" on friends, family, or unfortunate strangers.

4. He is afraid to get attached to anyone because he has learned that the people you love get killed, and he cannot face that pain again. He may make an exception for his children (because they cannot divorce him), but that will be instinctual and he will probably not be able to explain his actions.

5. He knows the military exists for a reason. The sad fact is that a military exists ultimately to kill people and break things. This was true of our beloved "Greatest Generation" warriors of WWII, and it remains true to this day. Technically, your warrior may well be a killer, as are his friends. He may have a hard time seeing that this does not make him a murderer. Although they may look similar at first glance, he is a sheepdog protecting the herd, not a wolf trying to destroy it. The emotional side of killing in combat is complex. He may not know how to feel about what he's seen or done, and he may not expect his feelings to change over time. Warriors can experiences moments of profound guilt, shame, and self-hatred. He may

have experienced a momentary elation at "scoring one for the good guys," then been horrified that he celebrated killing a human being. He may view himself as a monster for having those emotions, or for having gotten used to killing because it happened often. One of my Marines recommended On Killing by Dave Grossman, and I would pass that recommendation on.

6. He's had to cultivate explosive anger in order to survive in combat. He may have grown up with explosive anger (violent alcoholic father?) as well.

7. He may have been only nineteen when he first had to make a life and death decision for someone else. What kind of skills does a nineteen-year-old have to deal with that kind of responsibility? One of my veterans put it this way: "You want to know what frightening is? It's a nineteen-year-old boy who's had a sip of that power over life and death that war gives you. It's a boy who, despite all the things he's

been taught, knows that he likes it. It's a nineteen-year-old who's just lost a friend, and is angry and scared, and determined that some *%#& is gonna pay. To this day, the thought of that boy can wake me from a sound sleep and leave me staring at the ceiling."

8. He may believe that he's the only one who feels this way; eventually he may realize that at least other combat vets understand. On some level, he doesn't want you to understand, because that would mean you had shared his most horrible experience, and he wants someone to remain innocent.

9. He doesn't understand that you have a mama bear inside of you, that probably any of us could kill in defense of someone if we needed to. Imagine your reaction if someone pointed a weapon at your child. Would it change your reaction if a child pointed a weapon at your child?

10. When you don't understand, he needs you to give him the benefit of the doubt. He needs you also to realize that his issues really aren't about you, although you may step in them sometimes. Truly the last thing he wants is for you to become a casualty of his war.

*Regina Bahten has been practicing medicine for the past 24 years; the first twelve were as a primary care doctor...she then cross-trained as a psychiatrist. She has been honored with the friendships of many veterans over those years, whose influence led to her decision to accept a commission in the National Guard at the age of 48. For the past three years she has worked as an outpatient psychiatrist with the Veterans' Administration in Las Vegas, primarily with veterans of the current conflicts.

Read more at SpouseBUZZ.com:
http://spousebuzz.com/blog/2012/07/combat-vetera-wants-you-to-know.html#ixzz22R9x86KR

About the Authors

<u>Dr. Bridget C. Cantrell</u>: In 2004 and 2008 Dr. Bridget Cantrell was appointed as the Outstanding Female Non- Veteran for her service to veterans by the Governor's Veterans Affairs Advisory Committee and the Washington State Department of Veterans Affairs.

In 2008 Dr. Cantrell and her co-author Vietnam veteran, Chuck Dean were honored by receiving the "Erasing the Stigma Leadership Award" from the Didi Hirsch Mental Health Center in Los Angeles, California for their work with PTSD in veterans community and with our current service members. She is the President/CEO of Hearts Toward Home International, a charitable non-profit organization dedicated to the recovery and reintegration of trauma survivors.

Hearts Toward Home International has been recognized as the 2008 Best of Bellingham Award in the Non-profit Charitable Organization category by the U.S. Local

Business Association (USLBA). She was a finalist in 2013 for the Professional Woman of the Year in Whatcom County. Dr. Cantrell's primary work encompasses therapeutic counseling for war veterans and their families. With a Doctorate of Philosophy in Clinical Psychology, Bridget is a licensed Mental Health Counselor in the State of Washington, and a Nationally Board Certified Mental Health Counselor. She currently works as one of a small number of specially selected and trained Washington State Department of Veterans Affairs PTSD Specialists.

Presently, she provides mental health services to active duty troops from all branches of the military, including Reservists, National Guard, their leaders and family members.

This work focuses on providing effective tools for military personnel to readjust after experiencing the impact of combat exposure, trauma, family deployment stress and many other readjustment issues after service overseas.

Dr. Cantrell also trains first responders (law enforcement, firefighters, EMTs, hospital personnel, etc.) to better understand their role in the success of our warriors with whom they come in contact. She works with educational institutions and perspective employers to assure that our veterans are treated fairly and with the care and respect they deserve in order to succeed in the civilian sector.

Bridget is a member of Traumatic Stress Specialists. Currently she sits on the board for several veteran advocacy groups. She travels extensively conducting her workshops on combat stress for the military and their families throughout the European and Pacific duty assignments. She has authored many books available at bridgetcantrell.com and Amazon.com.

Headquartered in the Pacific Northwest she is also a Licensed Real Estate Broker for Weichert Realtors/Vanson Associates in the State of Washington and also finds this work very rewarding.

Chuck Dean: Chuck Dean was one of the first 300 regular Army paratroopers to be deployed to the Vietnam War in 1965, and as a result of that experience his voice, through writing and lecturing, has been heard loud and clear for decades on the transitional challenges experienced by returning veterans. He is the author of several books including the bestsellers "Nam Vet: Making Peace with Your Past", and "Down Range: To Iraq and Back". His latest fiction novels "Some Came Home" and "Inside Shadows" are sharp depictions of the struggles and triumphs war veterans encounter when their war is over. In 2008 Chuck was awarded the prestigious Hirsch Foundation Leadership Award in Los Angeles for his writing and work with veterans and their families. He served eight years as the National Chaplain of the 173rd Airborne Brigade Association, and now lives in Las Vegas, NV., and is a columnist for The Vegas Voice magazine.

For additional orders place inquiries and orders at:

Hearts Toward Home International
(an IRS approved 501c (3) public charity)
1050 Larrabee Avenue Suite 104,
PMB 714
Bellingham, Washington 98225-7367

(360) 714-1525

<u>This book is available on Amazon.com in both hard copy and digital (Kindle) formats.</u>

Other Recommended Reading by these Authors: (All can be found on www.Amazon)

"Nam Vet: Making Peace with Your Past"
Chuck Dean

"Some Came Home: A Story of Returning"
Chuck Dean

"Clandestine Hurt: The Revealing and Healing of Covert Pain"
Bridget C. Cantrell, Ph.D.

"Through the Woods and Over the Hill: The Aging of America's Warriors"
Bridget C. Cantrell, Ph.D.

"Souls Under Siege: The Effects of Multiple Deployments; and How to Weather the Storm"
Bridget C. Cantrell, PhD.

51494321R00116

Made in the USA
San Bernardino, CA
24 July 2017